DECORATING IS FUN!

DECORATING IS FUN!

HOW TO BE YOUR OWN DECORATOR BY DOROTHY DRAPER

WITH LINE CUTS AND HALFTONE ILLUSTRATIONS

POINTED LEAF PRESS, LLC.

PRINTED IN CHINA

10 9 8 7 6 5 4 3 2 1

LIBRARY OF CONGRESS NUMBER: 2006930818

ISBN-13: 978-0-9777875-1-7

ISBN-10: 0-9777875-1-6

To
My Mother and Father
Susan and Paul Tuckerman
The best amateur planners I know, who after more than fifty years of
married life, secretly long to build still another house
and to whom plans and decorations
are an unending fascination, delight and challenge,
this little book is dedicated with love,
gratitude and admiration.

INTRODUCTION

BY CARLETON VARNEY

It may seem farfetched that a book about interior design published on the eve of World War II could still be relevant and useful. But herein lies proof of the enduring genius and timeless style of Dorothy Draper. Though her tone in *Decorating Is Fun! How To Be Your Own Decorator* is lighthearted, her message is serious: she believed that anyone could have a comfortable and cheerful home if one followed her principles.

Mrs. Draper's book has stood the test of time because she did not dictate a one-size-fits-all style, although she was fond of certain motifs such as black-and-white checkerboard floors, bright floral chintzes, wide-striped wallpapers hung above a chair rail, and sky-blue ceilings. Mrs. Draper believed in individuality and she encouraged readers to consider their own needs, tastes, and budgets to make the most of their homes. With contagious enthusiasm and optimism, she offered advice about every element that goes into making a home, from hanging pictures and choosing paint colors to the correct size for lampshades and the importance of doorknockers.

The basic elements required for decorating a home have not changed in the last six decades, which is why Dorothy Draper has become a legend and an American icon. Certainly, that was not Dorothy Tuckerman Draper's goal in 1925, when she opened her first decorating business, Architectural Clearing House, which would later become Dorothy Draper & Company Inc., America's oldest established and continually operated design and decorating firm. Nevertheless, Mrs. Draper was an influential and unstoppable professional who helped turn interior design into a bona fide business. It wasn't easy for the tall, socially prominent woman who was raised in exclusive Tuxedo Park, New York, to become a force in the male-dominated design world and to win commissions for real estate developments, hospitals, resorts, clubs, automobiles, airplanes, and grand residences in the city, country, and abroad. But with her combination of genteel grit and innate good taste, she managed to pave the way for generations of women in the decorating profession.

Mrs. Draper's willingness to share her expertise and modus operandi with the masses through her books (and the columns she wrote for *Good Housekeeping* magazine in the 1940s) established her reputation as the country's authority on interior design. She is, without question in my mind, responsible for teaching America that the creation of a well-planned and beautifully decorated home is a worthwhile goal. I believe, as she did, that home is the center of our world, a place that should be filled with cheerful color where our families and friends feel relaxed and happy.

I have been president of the firm Mrs. Draper founded for more than forty years and our staff of architects, decorators, and space planners continues to create interiors that are based on the concepts in this book, which our firm has decided to reissue in conjunction with Pointed Leaf Press. Amazingly, Mrs. Draper's ideas are as practical as they were in 1939. A few years ago, *Entertaining Is Fun!*, with its original polka-dot jacket, was also reissued and it struck a chord with a new generation of men and women who wanted guidance on the art of being a great host or hostess. I expect that *Decorating Is Fun!*, in its original striped dust jacket, will be greeted with equal enthusiasm, for its pages contain many Dorothy Draper secrets, including the most important one of all: decorating well is easier than you think.

As I worked directly with Mrs. Draper and oftentimes traveled to installations with her, many people ask me: What was she really like? Was she a tough boss? Was she demanding in the office? Did she have lots of famous friends? What was her apartment in the Carlyle like? Did she dress fashionably? Was she fun to be with? I am always happy to answer these personal questions, for there are many erroneous tales about America's favorite decorator.

Dorothy Draper was a lady, from the top of her coiffured head to the tip of her polished shoes. She was polite but never reticent when it came to expressing her opinions, nor do I think she was oblivious to what was happening in the world around her. Nevertheless, she was, in many ways, a lady who lived in her own flower-filled ivory tower, often unaware of what others thought about design and decorating. She marched to her own drummer and single-mindedly set about achieving her goals.

Mrs. Draper was always fun to travel with. On our visits to the Greenbrier, the grand resort in West Virginia that she magnificently brought back to life in 1948 and continued to tweak and refresh throughout the remainder of her career, she would fastidiously sweep through the public spaces, making notes of what needed to be changed, painted, corrected. The Greenbrier was her baby; she knew every corner of the resort and cared a lot about each corner as well. When Mrs. Draper spent the evening at the Greenbrier nightclub, the Old White, the band would always strike up "The Hills of West Virginia." She enjoyed dancing but never stayed up too late. Though she never wore couture dresses, she did frequently shop at Bonwit Teller, the elegant Fifth Avenue department store then located directly across the street from our offices at 5 East 57th Street.

As far as being a tough boss, I would say yes and no. Mrs. Draper liked what she liked and would often come by each designer's desk to supervise and oversee what was being drafted. The seal of approval on a drawing was always "DD-OK." That meant "ready to go." Mrs. Draper was an extremely neat person in the office. Her desk pads were always placed exactly how she wanted them, and no secretary would ever dare to change their position because Mrs. Draper would always know.

I believe that Dorothy Draper was born with a magical talent. She was self-taught, as she grew up in a time when there were no schools of decorating and design and women were discouraged from having careers. Just as the Broadway legend Ethel Merman, one of my clients, possessed the natural ability to sing without amplification so that theatergoers in the third balcony could hear her, Mrs. Draper had a gift for reimagining any space as bright, cheery, and chic. Both women became major stars despite the fact that neither had any professional training.

The royalties received from this book will go toward the Dorothy Draper Scholarship Fund at the University of Charleston in West Virginia, a university close to Mrs. Draper's beloved Greenbrier. The fund will make it possible for an aspiring interior designer to learn the craft of decorating.

This reissue of *Decorating Is Fun!* includes original sketches and photographs from the archives of Dorothy Draper & Company Inc. Mrs. Draper's legacy is now accessible to all, and as this book suggests, her classic ideas and designs will endure through times to come.

Everyone always wants to know if there is a short cut to good decorating, and, in fact, there is. The following seven building blocks were among Mrs. Draper's favorite tools, and now you can use them, as I have, to create rooms that are polished, exuberant, and timeless.

1. Install a black-and-white marble floor—18-inch squares, please—in your foyer, living room, dining room, wherever. Make sure the black and white tiles are very clean and free of veining as much as possible, and definitely make certain that the marble squares are laid on the diagonal.

2. Install a white-painted dado and a white-painted chair rail—a requirement of rooms with the Dorothy Draper look. Use the "snowiest" white paint you can find.

3. Paint the ceilings a Thomas Jefferson pale aqua blue. Mrs. Draper liked people to look up and see the sky in her interiors.

4. Above the chair rail, use a clear Dorothy Draper color, like her favorite aqua blue, soft yellow, or neutral pale pink. Or, as she often did, choose a striped wallpaper in a rich hunter green and white of a 3- or 5-inch width. Sometimes in really large spaces, the stripes would be 15 inches wide.

5. Find a happy, full-blown, flowery chintz for the draperies and upholstery in a room that features stripes. Mrs. Draper believed stripes were decorating's common denominator and that stripes and a flowery chintz were a romantic combination. Don't think that green and white stripes belong only on Ascot awnings. Mrs. Draper used the stripes on window shades as well.

6. A Dorothy Draper room always required some touches of black. These could be lampshades, a Chinese-style coffee table, a pair of black-lacquer or porcelain end tables, or simply a black-lacquer box.

7. Put braided trim on comfortable chairs and sofas (Mrs. Draper loved fringe). Don't hang a single curtain without giving it an edge or two of handsome braiding or long bullion fringe, maybe 6 to 8 inches long. Big braided tie backs are also a must.

I believe that all of us are born with the potential to create a happy world filled with color, charm, and caring. I hope none of us ever forget to appreciate and share our blessings.

Carleton Varney
New York
July 2006

PREFACE

BY MRS THEODORE ROOSEVELT, JR

THIS is a truly delightful book that I wish every woman could read. For years people have been decorating their homes on a "Safety First" principle. The result is that hundreds and thousands of houses and apartments have walls of a "good neutral tan" and sets of furniture covered in some stuff that "goes with everything." These homes are so alike that their owners would seem to have no individuality whatsoever.

As a matter of fact, every woman in her secret heart believes herself to be a potential interior decorator, but usually when she gets started she loses her nerve. She is too easily influenced by what a salesman tells her is correct. She becomes confused by the great variety of materials that confront her when she shops. She loses confidence, becomes timid, and falls back on the drab and mediocre because she is afraid of doing wrong.

Dorothy Draper, stylist, industrial designer and one of the great authorities on decoration, tells you how to avoid all this. She tells you how to shop. She tells you how to use color and get effects you would never have dared try on your own and how to freshen up a commonplace room with smart, inexpensive little touches. She tells you not to despair if your living room is the wrong shape or you are obliged to live with a hideous set of parlor furniture that belonged to Great-aunt Sarah. She explains that comfort for your menfolk is the first essential, and shows why there is no reason this cannot exist in a lovely room.

Her suggestions are practical in the extreme whether you live in one room or twenty. As you experiment with them you will find yourself thinking and contriving in a way you would never have believed possible. Best of all, you can do it on your budget. If you cannot afford expensive fabrics or elaborate decorations, don't give it a second thought. You can, after reading this book, achieve miracles by using some of Dorothy Draper's ideas plus your own rapidly growing ingenuity.

Last year we built a house at Oyster Bay. We have wandered all over the world, and have accumulated a vast number of possessions on our travels. We never had money enough to buy really fine jades or porcelains, but we always managed to pick up things that to us were enchanting. We have scrolls and paintings from Tibet, primitive carvings from the mountains of Luzon, great strips of embroidery in glowing colors from Szechuan, painted wood figures from Cambodia and dear knows what besides. Our problem was to use all these because we love them, and yet keep our house from looking like a junk shop.

If *Decorating Is Fun!* had been published at that time it would have saved me many a headache. In this book you will find the solution to many of the problems we had to solve by trial and error. All you need is courage and daring backed up by common sense.

Dorothy Draper has been a friend of mine for many years. She has always had an extraordinary flair for achieving comfort and charm in whatever house she has lived in. She believes, and I thoroughly agree with her, that a house to be really a home should reflect all the various interests of every member of the family. Decorating is not apart from life but is a part of living itself. Life was meant to be happy and gay. Dorothy Draper shows you how happiness and gaiety can start right in your own home.

CONTENTS

xvi

PART II

HALFTONE ILLUSTRATIONS

PART I

1

HOW TO GET STARTED

A Decoration of Independence

Hᴀᴠᴇ ʏᴏᴜ ever considered how much pure stuff and nonsense surrounds this subject of interior decoration? Probably not. Almost everyone believes that there is something deep and mysterious about it or that you have to know all sorts of complicated details about periods before you can lift a finger. Well, you don't.

This is a book about how to have a good time decorating. If you want to be grim and serious about it don't read another word, for what I have to say is not for you. I don't believe there is any rule in the game that can't be broken.

Of course there is a certain amount of knowledge that will help you—a few principles of balance, proportion and restraint (as in life). Otherwise decorating is just sheer fun: a delight in color, an awareness of balance, a feeling for lighting, a sense of style, a zest for life and an amused enjoyment of the smart accessories of the moment.

By this I don't in any way mean to brand the study of period furnishings as stuff and nonsense. It is one of the most fascinating subjects in the world. You may find it so enticing that you will want to go into it thor-

3

oughly. If that's the case, you can spend many exciting hours in the museums or in the public library studying the true source material of our modern way of living.

Decorative styles are, after all, simply indications of a manner of living. The Victorians turned out stiff, unyielding furniture to fit stiffly corseted, unyielding figures. Louis Quinze chairs were made with very low arms to accommodate the enormous full skirts affected by the ladies of the day. (If you like to pick up a bit of knitting or sewing in the evening you may find a Louis Quinze chair will become your pet for just as practical a reason—it gives such freedom for elbow action.)

You may discover, through your own researches, that the styles of one certain period attract you so strongly that they seem to be designed just for you. In this case you will probably want to become a purist—you may want a room that grows up around Biedermeier furniture, Regency, Italian, French, or Chinese Chippendale pieces. You will probably also become very learned in your subject without even noticing that it is happening.

But if you are just a woman who wants her home to be a source of pride and delight to her, you need not be awed by the learned ones. You can spin your own web and make it very beautiful indeed.

Your home is the backdrop of your life, whether it is a palace or a one-room apartment. It should be honestly your own—an expression of your personality. So many people stick timidly to the often uninspired conventional ideas or follow some expert's methods slavishly. Either way they are more or less living in someone else's house.

I'm sure we have all seen rooms that, while they were undeniably beautiful, left us uneasy. "It's lovely," we say, "but I wouldn't want to live in it."

That just isn't our room no matter how happy it may make its owner. Sometimes even the owner will seem restless and out of place in her own living room. On the other hand, there is nothing as satisfying, nothing as friendly, as a house that seems graciously filled with the definite aura of its owner's personality.

I don't believe there is a woman alive who doesn't want this to be true of her home or who doesn't feel a real glow when some stranger says spontaneously, "Oh, what a lovely room." No woman really enjoys feeling apologetic about her home. No one really likes having to answer some friend's tactful criticism by saying, "Oh yes—that table. I know it doesn't look well there, but it was given to us by Aunt Martha."

We usually do nothing about Aunt Martha's table because we don't realize we *can* do anything that won't involve too much expense or expert advice. Neither of these objections is valid.

A home that is just what you really want is within your reach, whether you are a bride starting from scratch or someone who must make the best of what you have. Having to make the best of what we have is true of most of us—so true, in fact, that I have given the bride a chapter all to herself later on. Brides alone are in that enviable position for which the tired lady longed after she had been shopping all day for a new hat to go with last winter's coat. When she got home she sighed, "Oh, to be naked —with a checkbook!"

However, the very first thing you need doesn't cost a penny. And it is the first, by the way, of those fundamental principles I mentioned before.

Courage

YOU NEED COURAGE to experiment, courage to seek out your own taste and express it, courage to disregard stereotyped ideas and try out your own. Redecorating your living room in some new, enchanting color, or moving great-grandmother's wing chair from the right-hand side of the fireplace to the left may sound easy. Actually it is as drastic a psychological change as it is for a man to change jobs or for a woman to change husbands. I know a very conservative English bulldog who barks furiously if the furniture is disarranged. Many of us feel just that way although we are unconscious of it.

But courage doesn't mean recklessness. Before you can become your own decorator you must first become a critic. Before you make any decisions look the field over carefully. Take inventory of what the market has to offer and, above all, explore your own taste.

Your equipment is simple. For your journey of exploration all you need is a comfortably large bag (a laundry bag will do nicely), a pair of scissors, and an assortment of large filing envelopes. Hang the laundry bag on a closet door and use it for large samples. Use the scissors to clip anything that appeals to you out of the magazines and papers and file them in the envelopes. (At the end of this book you will find a list of magazines and books that I think are helpful.)

When you're out shopping never be afraid to ask for a snip of this or a snip of that. If you see a color that arrests your attention take a sample home with you. It doesn't matter whether it is burlap or felt, bath toweling or bed ticking, satin or velvet—it's the color that matters.

After you have done a certain amount of this snipping and snooping you will be surprised how it has intensified your own likes and dislikes. Certain colors will actually seem to warm you. Certain designs will delight you instantly. And other combinations, no matter how graceful or charming, will leave you cold. In other words, you will have found a key to a world of color and design that is peculiarly your own.

Don't be in the least disturbed by trends or fashions, or anyone else's advice. They are probably wrong. Be critical—never humble.

If you happen to go away for the week end—or even if you have just spent a few hours in a movie and so are temporarily removed from your daily life—stop as you re-enter your house and look about you. Try to see your rooms as if you were a total stranger seeing them for the first time and decide whether they satisfy all the new discoveries you've been making about your own taste. If they don't, try to put your finger on the reason. Perhaps it is color.

Color

COLOR, after you have your courage to experiment well in hand, is the next important fundamental.

The Drab Age is over. Color is coming into its own again. Until very recently people were literally scared out of their wits by color. Perhaps this was a hangover from our Puritan ancestors. But whatever the reason, browns, grays and neutrals were the only shades considered "safe." Now we know that lovely, clear colors have a vital effect on our mental happiness. Modern doctors and psychiatrists are convinced of this. Fantastic as it may sound, the doctors in many big department stores actually urge the salesgirls (who must wear unrelieved black all day) to carry bright-colored handkerchiefs and wear cheerful shades in their underclothes.

The picture of a harassed salesgirl, in the middle of the Christmas rush, dashing off into a corner to cheer herself up by a quick peek at a flame-colored petticoat may be pretty far-fetched, but it is certainly true that muddy, indeterminate colors can depress us. Be sure your colors are honest, fresh and clear. By honest colors I do not necessarily mean bright shades. A light powder blue is just as valuable as dark dahlia red as long as it isn't wishy washy. Clear fresh splashes of color can do more for a room than any other one thing. So much, in fact, depends on your harmony of color that Chapter Three of this book is devoted exclusively to it.

And hand in hand with color goes our next fundamental:

Balance or Size

THE PROPORTIONS of your room, the balance of your arrangements, the size of your furniture and accessories—all are almost desperately important. Many people have sensitive eyes when it comes to color, but so many are unawake when it comes to line. We have all seen, so many times, a woman whose dress is a beautiful shade but so badly cut for her particular figure that she completely lacks style. Just the same thing may be true of your house.

One room may be too long, another too small and high. Your sofa may be so bulky that it dwarfs the rest of the furniture in the living room. The windows in the bedroom may be so narrow and close together that they give the room a cross-eyed look. Your end tables may be just that inch or two too high that makes them look like storks. Your lamps may be of such varying heights that they give the effect of a roller coaster as your eye follows them around the room.

The solution to all these woes is not to burn the house down or put up with them, as most people believe. There are several simple decorative tricks that will disguise that bulky sofa, widen your living room and give the illusion of space between those cross-eyed windows. The tricks are not difficult once your eye has seen the faults. We will take them all up later on, in detail, in the chapter on Structural Backgrounds.

After Color and Balance we come to the next fundamental. It is the one I consider the best fun of all to shop for.

Smart Accessories and Details

ALL WOMEN KNOW how very important their clothes accessories are. It is just as disastrous to have the wrong accessories in your room as it is to wear sport shoes with an evening dress.

It may be that a new frame on that old picture would change its whole appearance. Junky knickknacks that you don't really like have a mysterious way of collecting themselves in your living room. They require a firm hand. Your ash trays and cigarette boxes should be just as decorative as they are useful. Your lampshades can make or break a room. Lamps, as a matter of fact, are just as important to the final dress of your room as is your Easter bonnet to your spring outfit.

It will always be these details of your room that will give it distinction. They will also lead the way to the last important fundamental.

Comfort

No ROOM can be called perfect unless it has real comfort. It must be livable for *you*. It must meet graciously every requirement you make of it. A room might be just right for a smart young woman who goes out a great deal and favors delicate colors and white furniture in her home. That same room, no matter how charming, would be miserably unsuitable for a hearty family who keep a great Dane and two growing boys to romp with him and like to play backgammon in the living room after dinner.

Plan your room for the people who live in it. Think of their habits as you arrange or rearrange your furniture. There are a few hard-and-fast rules about this arrangement which should be obeyed for the sake of balance. But they are very few, and otherwise you are free to experiment.

If you are the sort of person who likes to glance up from a book and out of the window, by all means place your pet armchair by that window. There's no law that says it can't turn its back on the whole room if you want it to. A room that is really comfortable for you will be the room that is most becoming to you. We've all seen rooms that look charming but are awfully unsatisfactory to stay in. "It doesn't look lived in," we say restlessly. And that's probably the whole trouble. It wasn't planned to be lived in. It lacks real comfort.

Without benefit of technical knowledge or mumbo jumbo, we have found five most powerful friends to guide us. Here they are:

> Courage
> Color
> Balance
> Smart Accessories
> Comfort

If we follow where they lead we may create homes that are not only beautiful, but capable of opening new doors for us, just as they did for some real women I happen to know. I shall tell their personal stories every so often throughout this book (usually at the end of the particular chapters where they seem most appropriate).

A decorator often learns as much about the private lives and intimate problems of her clients as does the family doctor! This may seem strange but it's really not. Decoration can't be divorced from living or it's not sound decoration.

So I offer you my little tales—or case histories—for what they may be worth in the light of your own problem. Naturally I've made up false names for everyone and I won't deny that in one or two instances I've combined two similar experiences to make one. But on the whole they are taken from life.

CASE HISTORY OF A COUNTRY WREN WHO TURNED INTO A CITY SPARROW

Cheerful little Mrs White had lived all her life in a pleasant country village. When her husband's business brought them to a large city she really didn't think she could stand it. The apartment they selected seemed so airless, so dark, so shut in. Actually it was perfectly comfortable but Mrs White had never realized how much she would miss her garden, or the trees along the roads and the birds. She grew positively mopey, didn't want to go out, and began a subtle undermining of her husband's enthusiasm for his new position.

When she realized that she was actually trying to hold back her husband's career just so she wouldn't have to live in the city she pulled herself together.

Her living room, to which she had paid very little attention, faced south and had a large, old-fashioned bay window. She had a carpenter set up a real latticework on either side of the entrance to the window. It didn't shut out any light or air and actually improved the balance of the room which the bay window had thrown off. To increase the effect she also had the carpenter build a sort of very high doorsill right across the entrance to the window. This partition stood up from the floor about six inches and was three inches wide, so you had to step over it to get into the window space. She laid black linoleum on the floor in front of the window and scattered real yellow pebbles all over it She covered the spaces between the window sections and also the ceiling over the window with sheet mirror. Then she put two ceiling-height rubber plants at either side, and placed low-growing plants on the floor in pots. At each window she placed low stands of bulbs where they would get the sun. In the middle she hung a lovely old English bird cage with two happily married bullfinches in it.

Now Mrs White likes her sunny little garden almost better than the one she left behind in the country. It flourishes all year round, and it's such a challenge to see what strange blooms she can raise in her stands.

CASE HISTORY OF A YOUNG LADY WHO WAS LONELY

Isabel Smart came to a big city to make her fortune. Since she was just beginning this interesting task she lived in a tiny, dreary little room. It looked much too much like a bedroom to permit entertaining, and it wasn't the sort of place that invites dropping in anyhow.

Isabel met several young men, and they would occasionally take her to a movie or to a restaurant for dinner. But not nearly often enough. The sort of girl who must always be taken somewhere and not brought home until it's time to say good night is expensive for young men who have just started making their fortunes too.

Isabel finally decided that she was tired of being "on the town" all the time. She was bright as a copper penny so she rolled up her sleeves and went to work.

She spent one Saturday afternoon tinting the nondescript walls of her room with clear yellow water-wash paint, which is inexpensive and simple to apply. Then she recklessly discarded the head- and footboards of her bed and kept just the box spring and mattress. The ideal thing would have been to have a carpenter attach very short legs to each corner of the box spring. But for the time being Isabel just braced up each corner with a brick apiece, and gave it a fitted cover that reached to the floor. Zipper covers of the same material for her bed pillows turned it into a couch.

She spent the next Saturday afternoon in the department stores and came home with a real bargain—a fairly inexpensive chintz that was a delightful copy of an old English pattern. With this she made new curtains and a loosely fitting slip cover for her big, comfortable chair.

She painted her dresser exactly the same color as the walls and exchanged the toilet articles that had littered it for a big Lowestoft bowl (given her by her mother) full of fruit.

A decorative though inexpensive screen in one corner of the room concealed a tiny electric stove. A big kitchen mixing bowl with a tight-fitting lid served as a sort of icebox that could be filled at the corner drugstore when she wanted to serve drinks. (Ice will keep a surprisingly long time in anything closed. Or, if you have a little more money than Isabel Smart, you can buy thermos containers that will keep ice twenty-four hours. They cost around $10.)

The whole job had cost Isabel just the sort of work that is stimulating to do and under $20 in actual cash. And it has been worth it ten times over. Isabel has a home now—a place that invites you to sit down for a cup of coffee after the theater or just the place to go when you want to listen to the Saturday afternoon baseball game in comfort. She has more friends—and more beaux—than she knows what to do with.

CASE HISTORY OF A LADY WHO GOT HER OWN WAY REGARDLESS

Like many women who tend to be Brunhildas in their build Mrs Valentine has a secret passion for delicacy. When she redecorated her living room last year she let it all out with a bang. This would have been splendid if Mrs Valentine had lived all alone, but she doesn't. Mr Valentine is a big, rangy fellow who doesn't say much but takes up a lot of space very comfortably. Johnny Valentine is going to be as big as his father some day and is at the awkward age.

Under the circumstances Mrs Valentine should have realized that the living room in her house is a community affair—and that she rates just one third of the consideration. Unfortunately, this never occurred to her.

She made herself a lovely pink-and-white room. White walls, a white floor, and a big, modern off-white rug started the picture. Pink curtains and upholstered satin furniture with pale pink-and-white stripes came next. She used a lot of crystal and glass throughout the room, and she selected end tables and lamps that definitely veered toward fragility. When she was finished her room was as charming as a baby chicken—and just about as perishable.

Even the upholstered chairs were on the small side. Mr Valentine tested them out gingerly and always felt as if he needed a shave when he sat down in one. Evenings in the Valentine household became more than a little tense, punctuated by small cries of alarm from Mrs Valentine.

"Johnny—watch that table!" or "Val, darling, *don't* knock your pipe out there—you're spattering!" interrupted any conversation.

It is possible that some day Mrs Valentine will wake up and realize that although she has a lovely room to look at, it doesn't live up to its name—"living" room. It deprives her family of that cardinal virtue: comfort.

When that day comes I hope she will transfer the whole thing to her bedroom where she can enjoy it to her heart's content. If she doesn't, I don't know just what will happen to her (except that she will be written up as a horrible example in a book like this). For Mr Valentine goes to the club now much more than he used to. And Johnny goes to the movies. Mrs Valentine spends a good many evenings alone, like one chocolate in a big, handsome bon-bon box. And so far she hasn't the least idea what has given her family the away-from-homing instinct.

2

BACKGROUNDS

Your Room in the Nude

I IMAGINE we have all known the thrill that comes when we walk into our brand-new, empty apartment, or house, just after we've signed on the dotted line, and before a single stick of furniture has been moved in. It must be much the same thrill that a painter feels when he sets up a new, empty canvas and starts to plan his picture. The longing to pitch right in, and turn that empty box into a room, is almost irresistible.

I even know one woman who used to while away the black hours when she had insomnia by designing, building and completely furnishing a whole house in her mind. She would say contentedly, at breakfast, "Well, I finished the sun porch last night." She told me the other day, however, that she has had to give up this pleasant habit and go back to counting sheep because she had so much fun and got so interested in her imaginary arrangements that she never *did* fall asleep.

Naturally, most of us are not confronted with a brand-new, empty house. We're already living in a settled one that we've decided to do something about. But since the easiest place to begin is the beginning, let's pretend that it's new and empty.

And since a house, or apartment, is after all just a succession of rooms, let's start with just one room. Whatever rules apply to that room will also apply to every other room in the house. Also, since this chapter devotes itself to backgrounds (the actual shell or framework of your room), whatever rules we pick up along the way are universal. They apply to any enclosed space that is lived in, whether it is a one-room city apartment, a sprawling old house in the country, or a palace on the Riviera.

The first step is always the same: visualize your room in the nude, waiting for you to hand it all its clothes. It is just an empty, plaster box, with openings for doors, windows and fireplace. It doesn't matter what style of furniture you're going to put into it, that shell of your room is very important. Just as if it were a person, you can spend a fortune on its clothing and if its posture is bad, or its figure ugly, it won't look like much.

Unfortunately, very few rooms are perfectly balanced—beautifully proportioned. But just as a clever dressmaker can design your clothes to emphasize your good points and conceal the bad ones, so you can dress your room in a way that will flatter it.

The first thing to worry about is superfluous fussiness. Look around you for doodads. Is there an old-fashioned picture molding? Are the walls broken up into panels by molding strips? Is there a center chandelier with plasterwork around it? Are there too many wall lights, badly placed?

Before you make a single decision rip off every unnecessary doodad. Picture molding is never used nowadays. (Pictures are hung invisibly on special hooks purchased at any ten-cent store.) Unless you have a particularly beautiful chandelier which will be part of your decorative scheme you probably won't use that center light (except possibly in bed-rooms or halls). Very few modern houses use wall brackets any more. Your room will probably be lighted by lamps. Panels on the walls do nothing but break up the lines of the room and give it a choppy appearance.

When you have eliminated all the purposeless frills I guarantee you will heave a big sigh of relief at the restful simplicity of your framework.

The next thing to notice is the actual shape of your room. Is it long and narrow? Too low ceilinged? Too small for the height of its ceiling? Has it irregularities—one beam at one end of the ceiling and none at the other? Has it a jog in the wall somewhere? Are the windows evenly spaced and of the same size? Is the fireplace in the center of its wall? Are the doors well placed—or is there a door at one end of a wall and nothing to balance it at the other end? Are the radiators well placed?

Here are the main things to check:

1. Shape of the box—length, width, height
2. Balance of doors and windows
3. Position of fireplace, or other center of attraction
4. Irregularities—odd beams, jogs in wall, alcoves, etc.
5. Position and balance of radiators

Now you can really plan a campaign against your room's structural defects. If your room is rented, and many of your ideas involve actual carpentering work, this is the time to plan a campaign against the land-lord too. One thing landlords seem surprisingly amenable about, for instance, is moving radiators. I don't know why this is so, since they'll fight to the death on much less troublesome matters. Naturally, you'll get just as much out of the landlord as you possibly can, and then decide whether the other expenses are worth it to you when figured as part of the rent.

Irregularities

IF YOU HAVE a ceiling with one beam you may want to have a fake, matching beam installed for the sake of balance. You may want to install a door to balance another door, even though the new one is just a wall decoration. You may want to match one jog in the wall with another, though an irregularity in the wall can often be turned to advantage by building in a bookcase. Or, if the jog is so big that it really is an alcove, you can make it very attractive by giving it a decorative scheme all its own—placing the piano there, or the desk, or the dining table.

A Small High Room

IF YOUR ROOM is terribly small, but very high, as is the case in some old houses, you will notice that this gives a gloomy, boxlike effect. High ceilings are usually an asset—it is only when a room is really tiny that they aren't good. You'll want to make your room look as big as possible by your selection of its color scheme later on. (It should be simple in any small room.) Right now you may want to plan to use mirrors on one wall to make it seem larger. Or you may want to install a chair rail, which will always make a room seem lower. If you plan to paint the room, the part of the wall between the chair rail and the floor (called dado) can be painted a different color from the rest of the wall. If you prefer paper you will select a pattern that emphasizes horizontal lines.

If there is no cornice (the molded ornament that separates walls and ceiling) in a very high room, think seriously of having a carpenter supply one. It makes such a great difference. In a very high room this cornice should be painted the color of the ceiling—not of the walls. If your room happens to be a bedroom you can get the effect of a cornice by using a wide wallpaper border around the wall right under the ceiling.

A Low Room

IF YOUR ROOM IS LOW it isn't as serious, for a low room is usually cosy. But you can raise the ceiling considerably by the use of vertical lines. Make a mental note to consider striped wallpaper later on. Another trick is to carry the color of the walls, or the wallpaper, right over the cornice and ceiling. Or, if you want to be slightly startling, paint the ceiling shiny black. It will act almost as a mirror, and have the faraway look of a midnight sky.

A Narrow Room

IF A ROOM is too narrow for its length, plan to place a large mirror on its long wall. (See frontispiece.) Perhaps this mirror can go over the sofa or the fireplace, extending clear to the ceiling. Or you can mirror a whole wall, excluding of course the window spaces that occur in it. Even doors can be mirrored. The use of great sheets of mirror is definitely smart today and will probably be so for a long, long time. It does more for a feeling of spaciousness than anything else. And don't discard the whole idea because you remember how much that small, framed mirror cost, either. Sheet mirror is quite a different proposition and can be bought for as little as $1.75 per square foot. Flash mirror is even cheaper. (This is ordinary window glass painted black on one side so that it acts as a mirror even though it doesn't reflect accurately.)

A Bad Fireplace

MANY an otherwise pleasant room is ruined by a fireplace that is a towering horror. If you have a bad one, and don't feel like having the whole thing remodeled, plan to paint it the same color as the walls and it won't show up nearly as much. This holds good for any structural defect that you can't do anything about. If the fireplace facing is an ugly color this too may be painted the same color as the walls, or dead white, or shiny black.

Doors

THE DECORATION OF DOORS is something that most people ignore, and I'll discuss it in full in a later chapter. Right now you are just worried about whether your doors are well placed. If they're not, you'll decide now about having a fake, balancing door installed as I mentioned before. Or if your room is so broken up with too many doors that you're short of wall space, consider closing off a seldom-used door with a screen. The only trick about such a screen is to make sure that it is big enough to cover everything about the door, including the trim.

Windows

LET'S NOT WORRY about the details of dressing our windows now either. Their shape and placing is what counts at the moment. If you have any stained glass, be ruthless and get rid of it. It will just cut out light and look so out of place that it will bully your whole room.

If your windows are too narrow, make a note now that when you do select your curtains they should be hung outside the window trim, so that most of the folds will come on the wall instead of on the glass. They will immediately look wider. If you have two windows that are too close together hang the outside curtains beyond the window trim and the inside curtains normally.

If a window is too short hang the curtains very high from a valance fastened right on the wall above the window. This valance must come down and touch the window top and conceal the fact that this really *is* the window top. The valance can be made of wood, fabric, or mirror.

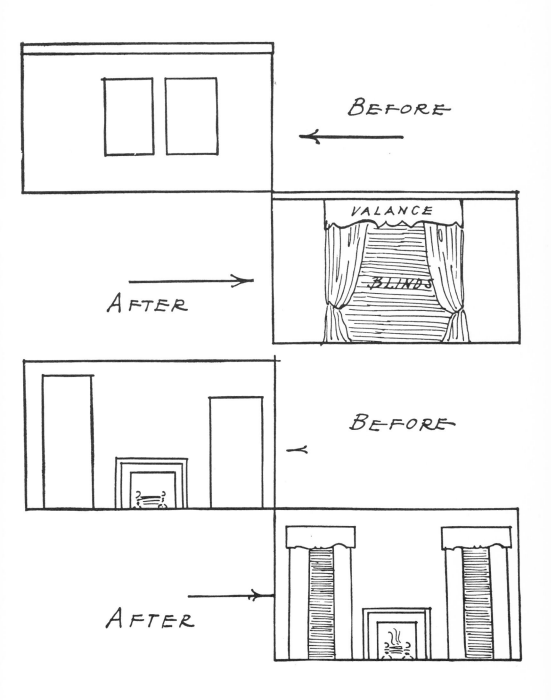

Then with your curtains falling from the high valance clear to the floor you will get an impression of a beautifully long window. If you use Venetian blinds plan to have them go all the way to the floor, too, even if the window does not. The only time you won't be able to do this is when there is a wide window seat.

When you have two windows on one wall that don't match in size the use of this all-concealing valance will make the smaller one seem just as big as the other. (If this sounds confusing I think the sketches will clear it up.)

Off-center Play

IF YOUR FIREPLACE is off-center, leaving a longer wall space on one side than on the other, remember that fact when you start to arrange your furniture. The best thing to do with your off-center fireplace is to set a good heavy piece of furniture, like a sofa, right opposite. Don't center the sofa on the wall, as you would normally do, or it will be out of line with the fireplace and look more higgledy-piggledy than ever. When you have lined up the sofa and the fireplace you can arrange the long end of your room as a square, or oblong, space with a balanced decorative scheme of its own. (The sketches on page 25 show you the right and wrong way to handle an off-center fireplace.)

After you've juggled the contours of your room around for a while, and decide on whatever bit of plastic surgery or deception is necessary, you aren't going to be able to resist thinking about wallpaper or paint much longer. And since they both should be considered in relation to your whole color scheme we'd better stop this chapter right now, for that is what the next one is about.

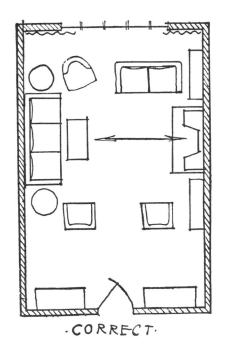

·CORRECT·

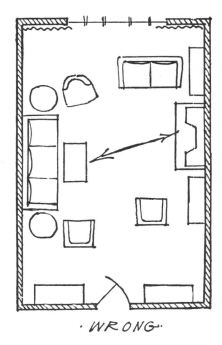

·WRONG·

CASE HISTORY OF A YOUNG LADY WITH A NICE SMALL HUSBAND

Young Mr and Mrs Lovelace had only been married six months and had been living at a hotel. Mrs Lovelace was awfully excited about their first apartment and dragged Mr Lovelace along to look at several possibilities. She found one that she loved in a remodeled private house in old Washington Square in New York. She was especially crazy about the big high-ceilinged living room. It had a beautiful white marble mantelpiece and Santo Domingan mahogany doors with silver knobs.

To her enormous disappointment Mr Lovelace was just lukewarm about it. As Mrs Lovelace stood in the vast, empty room excitedly shoving furniture around in her mind, Mr Lovelace wandered nervously about and finally went back to the kitchen. He hadn't any real objections to the apartment, just seemed uneasy.

Mrs Lovelace suddenly felt cross. When he came out of the kitchen again she stared at him resentfully. Of course he was wonderful and she loved him madly but why did he pull his head down into his shoulders that way and look so rabbity—and, well, just plain small? Suddenly a great light dawned. Mr Lovelace rattled around like one pea in a pod in this lovely big room—and that was why he didn't like it.

Mrs Lovelace thought it all over after they got back to their hotel. She loved the comfort of large rooms, particularly large living rooms. She took the apartment, and set about making that living room look as cozy, and as low ceilinged, as she possibly could.

She selected flowered wallpaper of a particularly warm, splashy pattern, and had the ceiling and cornice painted dusty pink instead of white. She placed low, two-shelf bookcases on either side of the fireplace in order to break up the wall with their horizontal line. She put big crystal vases filled with branches of rhododendron on the bookcases.

She made sure her lamps were not tall spindly ones, but big and solid. She used a valance at the top of her windows and looped her curtains. She bought low, comfortable upholstered furniture and had it loosely slip-covered to the floor—no leggy pieces that look taller than they are. She used oversized coffee tables; five feet six inches long, two feet six inches wide, and eleven and one half inches high.

When she was all finished and had lighted the fire, she had the most friendly room imaginable and Mr Lovelace was crazy about it. He put his feet on the coffee tables and felt as big as an ox. He had somehow seemed to grow a good two inches, and Mrs Lovelace thought he was wonderful.

3

COLOR

Your Magic Wand

I WISH there were one word in the English language that meant exciting, frightfully important, irreplaceable, deeply satisfying, basic and thrilling, all at once. I need that word to tell you how much your awareness of color means to you in decorating. It is the rock on which your house is built. Without a keen sense of color, without the ability to get real enjoyment and excitement out of lovely colors, we might as well quit right now. I firmly believe that nothing contributes so much to the beauty of this world as color. And, happily enough, I believe with equal conviction that every man, woman and child alive has within him a true instinct for color.

Sometimes that instinct has been neglected till it is rather deeply buried. But it is so easy to find it in yourself. I cannot overemphasize, even at the risk of sounding school-teacherish, the importance of finding it. When you have an awareness of color, then, and only then, can you make a picture to yourself of what you want to do.

Try to picture to yourself (grab your head in your hands like a Shakespearean actor if you want to) a cyclamen in the sunshine—the leaf

27

of a lily of the valley—white Easter lilies against a soft white wall—the pink inside of a sea shell—the silvery trunk of an old birch tree—the darkly shimmering greens on the back of a frog. Your imagination can paint pictures that can never be surpassed in oils.

Try the same technique on a room but go more slowly here, stopping after each new step so that the colors are glowing firmly in your mind.

A cherry-red carpet—dead-white walls—a sky-blue ceiling (take it easy, there, these are not just words). Cover all the upholstered furniture with yards and yards of gaily flowered chintz on a dead-white background—hang crisp, white muslin curtains with great big ruffles—place large plain glass vases full of laurel on the mantelpiece—light the fire—and before its shining fender put a white fox terrier wagging his tail at the flames.

That's a very pleasant room you've got there and you haven't worried about a thing except its color scheme! You got it without benefit of complicated color charts or hocus-pocus, too. I think most of the color charts you'll find in decorating books are ridiculous. No decorator—either professional or amateur—who is worth her salt really plans her color schemes from a card index file. The world is full of beautiful colors to choose from, and everyone has her own individual preferences. Select the loveliest colors you can find—throw them together—and your own taste, resourcefulness and independence will carry you through.

Above all, never be afraid of color. As I've said before, the day of drab, timid colors is past. We are all beginning to learn the magic of color —the glorious chance it gives us to turn a dreary room into something miraculous, and the relative cheapness with which the transformation of the whole feeling of a house may be brought about by its gay, fearless use.

Be open-minded in your selection of background color in particular.

Muddy-colored walls are nothing but a blight. So are undecided colors that compromise between tan and apartment-house cream, or between two greens until they become the so-called "Adam green," or between two blues until they become neither sea, sky nor good old cornflower.

There should never be any doubt about what your color has to say, whether it is a pale or a brilliant shade. It may be chalk blue, watermelon pink, lemon yellow, grass green, chocolate brown, café au lait, warm gray —anything on earth you like, just as long as it knows its own mind.

The fashionable names for different shades change so whimsically from year to year that I find it simpler to have my own names, and stick to them. There is usually something in food (like cranberry red), or in nature (sky blue) that will give you just the phrase you want. So don't be bothered if a saleswoman tells you haughtily, "Oh, that's not brick this year—it's terra cotta now." If it's the color of bricks you want you'll get it by asking for just that. And just be hard-boiled if they tell you that such and such a color isn't "fashionable" this year. There are always fads in colors, and my best advice is to ignore them unless they happen to appeal to you in spite of being in style.

Floors, walls and ceilings are the most important colors to worry about because there's so much of them.

Walls

A GOOD TRICK when you are considering wall colors is to get a large wall-paper sample (most shops give them away) which has the background color you want. Hang it on the wall until you find out whether you really like it. Then have your painter match that shade.

And here's a tip about painters. They are undoubtedly sterling characters but they have slapped on an awful lot of paint in their day and consequently are inclined to be a little unconcerned about getting just the shade you want. If you're doubtful that your painter has really turned the trick after the first half dozen samples, let them all dry. If possible, look at them in morning light, afternoon light and electric light. Don't let the painter use some different color for the ground coat as he's apt to do. And always remember that a small sample of any shade looks three times darker when it's all over the wall.

You can change an ill-advised chair cover without breaking the bank at Monte Carlo, but walls, ceilings and floors are much bigger fry. So it's well worth being fussy about them in the beginning.

If you prefer wallpaper to paint by all means get a good big sample, even if you have to pay for it and hang it on the wall for twenty-four hours before you buy the lot. I believe in extra large samples of every-thing, as a matter of fact. It never pays to take the expensive chance of trying to carry too much in your mind.

In a small house, or apartment, it is often a good idea to use exactly the same shade for all the walls. It doesn't chop up the final effect and make the whole space seem smaller, as varying colors are liable to do. It is even a good idea, in a very small room, to paint the furniture the same color as the walls. It will seem to melt right back into them and take up much less space.

The room pictured opposite page 32 used this color trick to excel-lent effect. It measured eleven and a half by nineteen feet. The color selected for walls, ceiling and woodwork was sky blue—a spacious shade. But there was no reason to stop there and leave heavy, dark furniture to make the room seem crowded. Even though some of it was mahogany the furniture was painted exactly the same color as the walls. Even the frames on the few pictures used were painted blue. The curtains, hung so effectively at the big window at the end of the room, were also blue of an identical shade. When they were reflected in the mirrored wall opposite them they made that wall seem to go on and on to twice its depth. The floors were painted white, and a deep white fur rug laid. The lamps were tall hurricane chimneys of glass, with pleated white shades. The bricks around the fireplace were painted mauve, and the fender and andirons shining chromium instead of brass. A collection of white flowered china which the owner happened to have, was hung over the fireplace and gave the place an added touch of individuality.

This color scheme shattered one old idea—that blue is always a "cold" color. Blue can be delicate and yet warm at the same time. The quality of this room was that of sparkling daintiness combined with spaciousness. At night it was really luminous. And all these effects could be directly traced to the use of color, repeated a thousand times in mirror.

Don't ever be afraid to use the same color throughout the house, provided you like it. Just as the main theme appears and reappears throughout a symphony, so you can carry one note of color through your whole house to beautiful effect. I don't mean that the color scheme in each room should be just alike—anything but. You just bind the whole thing together by light touches of the same shade.

For instance, if you have red curtains in your living room, you might have white walls in the hall with a red design stenciled on them. Then in your dining room you might place a rug of the same color. In your bedroom you would just strike the note lightly—put a red quilt, folded, on the end of the bed. Just for fun you could even paint the cellar stairs or the inside of your kitchen closets that same red.

In this way you can create a sort of intelligent "color continuity" that is very satisfying, and smart to boot.

ONE-ROOM APARTMENT
Before and After

THE PROBLEM   This is the same room pictured in the frontispiece which illustrates the manner in which the use of mirror makes the room seem larger. The second problem was to give the room the appearance of a charming living room in spite of the fact that it had to be turned into a bedroom at night.

THE SOLUTION   1. The sofa, opposite the fireplace, is a full-size single bed equipped with a comfortable box spring and mattress. Underneath the chintz slip cover that covers the mattress, the bed is completely made up—only the pillow and comforter need be put away in the drum table during the daytime.

2. Sheet mirror, placed on each side of the fireplace, widens the room. Notice, in particular, how the long simple curtains at the large window are reflected in the mirror and make the wall seem to go on and on.

3. The china used over the fireplace, and also on the opposite wall as well, is an unusually charming touch. (The owner of this apartment just happened to have a lovely set of china and had sense enough to make use of it. So often people have really beautiful things that are buried in the attic or hidden away.)

4. The large lamp in the foreground is made of a hurricane chimney wired by the local electrician and set on a base. The pleated shade is made of three tiers of white buckram. As the light shines through the different thicknesses it gives an effect of color even though the shade is white.

5. The two low stands on each side of the fireplace are useful as well as ornamental—one holds the radio and books and the other covers the radiator and houses magazines. (Notice that they are exactly the same height as the arm of the upholstered chair.)

6. The slip-covered chair is equipped with a wooden cleat on the floor that holds it firmly in position. (In a small room comfort depends so largely on order and balance—everything must stay exactly in its place.)

7. The floor of the room is painted white. The four white fur rugs were not nearly as expensive as they look—they cost only $4.50 each at a local department store and are just laid side by side on the floor.

8. The fireplace equipment—andirons, fender and tongs—is all chromium. (It is actually an old brass set, redone.)

9. Notice that the fireplace is very much off-center. In order not to give the whole room a lopsided appearance the sofa bed is placed directly *opposite* the fireplace instead of in the center of its wall.

10. The inside of the fireplace and the hearth are painted mauve (one of the colors on the china)—the only other note of color in an otherwise blue-and-white room. Walls, ceiling and all furniture are all clear sky blue.

11. The coffee table is well placed—but if it were slightly larger the final effect would be better.

32

Ceilings

MOST PEOPLE FORGET all about their ceilings and go right on painting them white or neutral. They can do almost as much for your room as a sunny or cloudy sky can do for the landscape under it. *Always* include them in your color plans. Your ceiling can be a contrast to your walls, or it can match some color in your wallpaper or your rug. It can be painted shiny black, or it can be covered with the same wallpaper you are using on the walls. Just don't treat it like a stepchild.

Floors

THE COLOR OF THE FLOOR is, of course, just as important as that of the walls or ceiling.

If you have wood floors the wisest thing is to have them stained a very dark brown and keep them waxed or polished. Whatever happens, don't let your painter give you light oak-shellacked floors. A floor should gleam softly, not hit you in the face with its glitter as does a light-shellacked floor. Or, if you go in for the pale-colored modern rugs, your oak floors can be bleached to a silvery gray with ammonia. (Your painter should be consulted on this process.)

White floors are unusually effective though I'll grant they mean plenty of scrubbing. Or floors can be marbled—pink, brown, white and yellow as a base for a pink room, perhaps.

The Color Scheme as a Whole

THE MAIN THING to remember is not to be afraid of a color combination you like because you think it is too extreme or hifalutin. It probably isn't at all. And it won't cost a cent more than a dull one. Chinese-red paint costs no more than mud-colored. Good taste costs no more than bad. In fact. it usually costs less. You don't have to pay yourself for your own taste as you sometimes do when you allow yourself to be saddled with someone else's preferences.

Just because floors, walls and ceiling are very important doesn't mean that you have to begin your whole color plan with them. You can start off anywhere you want just as long as you give them their due consideration.

Some people believe that the exposure of your room should influence your choice of colors. They talk about brightening a north room with warm colors and air-conditioning a south room with cold colors. I have never believed that colors can be split up autocratically into "warm" and "cold" groups. Nor do I think that you should let the exposure of your room boss you around. Choose your colors because you *like* them. Your own good sense will tell you that if you are decorating a bedroom the colors can be more delicate, more pastel in tone than those used in the living room. If you're planning a game room you will know that you can be more flamboyant—can use gay, startling color combinations that are in tune with the room's holiday spirit.

We'll prowl through a lot of living rooms, bedrooms, playrooms and kitchens in detail later on in this book. So right now, we'll just worry about basic color combinations that could be modified, by their accessories, to fit any sort of room.

These color schemes can grow out of anything you please. You may prefer to start with pure color combinations in mind—deep elephant gray, clear yellow and black, for instance. Then you might decide that the walls can carry the gray, the rugs and upholstery the yellow and the floor the black. Or you may start with something you already own that is a color you love: a length of chintz, or a favorite painting.

As soon as we get beyond the simple combination of floor, walls and ceiling, however, we come up against a problem that bothers many people. When we select our curtain colors, and our upholstered furniture, we must visualize a color on another color—a pattern on a pattern. We must know how a certain chair is going to look, not standing by itself in a vacuum, but against the background of the wall or curtains.

There are two ways of handling this. You can take your choice.

1. *An Exactly Matching Color Scheme*—one that weaves the same color through the whole room. The sky-blue room described earlier in the chapter is an example of this type of room. Everything in it was blue and white—ceiling, walls, curtains, furniture were all the same tone of blue. It was relieved only by pale touches of other colors that had the same intensity as the blue (the bricks around the fireplace were mauve). This sort of room is quiet in its effect. It is really a background for individuals.

2. *A Sharply Contrasting Color Scheme*—one that combines colors that set each other off. In a room of this type if you had a hunting-green carpet your upholstered chairs would have to be some other color that would show up sharply against that green. They might be sealing-wax red, or red-and-white stripes, or gaily flowered chintz, or black. They would definitely not be solid green. This room would also contrast pattern against solid color. If the curtains were of figured material the chairs would be solid color. If a flowered wallpaper was used the curtains would be plain.

Here are a few combinations that may appeal to you, or give you ideas of your own. I've divided them into the two types:

Matching Rooms

1. Walls: white
   Ceiling: palest pink

Carpet: possibly an Aubusson of palest blue-and-pink flowers on a creamy-white background

Curtains: white, lined with pale pink or pale blue

Slip covers: heavy white material to match curtains

2. Walls: hydrangea blue

Ceiling: hydrangea blue

Carpet: white fur rug, on a white floor

Curtains: hydrangea blue

Slip covers: white

(Chromium and glass accessories)

3. Walls: pale café au lait

Ceiling: shiny black

Carpet: clipped coffee-colored fur rug on shiny black floor, or all-over carpeting of coffee color

Curtains: café au lait with a big black fringe

Slip covers: café au lait to match curtains

(If there is a fireplace the mantel should be black. Accessories should be gold and white.)

4. Walls: palest green

Ceiling: white

Carpet: darker green

Curtains: same pale green as walls, but of a textured material

Slip covers: white chintz, with a green lily-of-the-valley design.

Contrasting Rooms

1. Walls: white

Ceiling: deep sky blue

Carpet: bright cherry red

Curtains: crisp white muslin

Slip covers: English chintz with bold red roses with dark green leaves on a dead-white background

2. Walls: deep elephant gray

Ceilings: same deep gray

Carpet: mustard yellow

Curtains: bright lemon yellow

Slip covers: same yellow as curtains

(A touch of Chinese-red lacquer should appear somewhere among the accessories.)

3. Walls: pine (or pine paper, or cork, or imitation pigskin leatherette)

Ceiling: white

Carpet: Irish green

Curtains: Hunting-pink felt curtains with matching wool fringe

Slip covers: chintz, or, if possible, black leather chairs.

(Gay hunting prints would be excellent on the walls.)

4. Walls: white paper with huge cabbage roses with dark green leaves

Ceiling: pale pink

Carpet: gray or green

Curtains: emerald green

Slip covers: striped green and white

Do remember, though, that these are just suggestions—not ironclad formulas. There really are no set rules about the use of color. Just don't be frightened into using dull colors or conventional combinations when you know you really like something else.

I don't believe in set rules about anything, for that matter. Here are a few that I find helpful—but I herewith cheerfully present them to you to be broken whenever you please:

A Few Tips for Color Tipplers

1. Remember that there is no such thing as a "correct" or "incorrect" color combination. First select a basic color that you really like.

2. Then decide whether you want to compose a room using just that color, relieved only by touches of other colors that blend softly because they are of the same intensity, or whether you want one that contrasts your basic color with another that sets it off. (I'll be honest and admit that the contrasting scheme is safer. A room that uses just one color may turn out beautifully, but it is more difficult to foresee the results.)

3. By all means, confine yourself to just a few colors in one room. Too many ideas are just as bad as none at all.

4. In the average room it's usually a good plan not to jumble your upholstery colors. Make all your slip covers of the same material. Get your contrast somewhere else.

5. Let your guiding principle be simplicity, both in design and color combinations. The whole trend of today is away from fussy, overcrowded effects.

And when you think you're all ready to start, gather the samples of every color you intend using in your room in one fist and ask yourself whether you would wear them all in one costume. If you wouldn't, don't ask your room to do it either.

CASE HISTORY OF A YOUNG LADY WHO WORE GLASSES

Miss Susan Silver lived until she was thirty-five years old with her mother. Her mother belonged to that fine old school that definitely knew its own mind. This meant that Miss Susan usually didn't. They lived with the mother's white Persian cat, and so many knickknacks that you didn't dare draw a deep breath in the living room for fear of blowing something off the tables.

When Mrs Silver died, Miss Susan missed the autocratic but dear old lady very much. But she finally woke up one morning filled with what was for her an unholy energy. When she banged her ankle sharply on one of the innumerable little footstools in the living room she said "Damn," and decided to do the whole room over.

The only trouble was that when she began to select its new color scheme she got panicky. "Brown is safe," she thought, and told the painter to do the walls a washed-out sort of buff. Then she bought a big, dark rug that they told her was "plum." She ordered a plain brown chair in a different store—thought they were the same shade, although she didn't have a sample of the rug with her. An enthusiastic salesman sold her a mustard-colored sofa (probably to get rid of it), and she thought she could use her mother's old mahogany.

When all the new things were assembled in the living room she tried to talk herself into a state of excitement. After all, she had never owned anything that was all hers before in her life. So you can't blame her if she felt bitterly chagrined as she sat in the big brown chair, stared at the plum-colored rug and mustard sofa and just plain didn't like them.

She sat there quietly like a thin brown ghost for about half an hour. When she got up her disappointment had made her reckless. She remembered a photograph of a lovely room that she had cut out of *Vogue* a couple of years before, and scrabbled through her desk until she found the description. She couldn't possibly have created the room herself—but there it was, and she wanted it.

She marched right back to the stores and told them to take away the plum-colored rug and the sofa and the chair. Then she discarded everything else in the living room except some lovely old engravings and a comfortable wing chair.

She called the painter back again, and, although he obviously thought she was crazy, she made him do the whole room over a soft, faded pink. Then she hung curtains of the same shade, and had them lined with red-and-white striped satin. She bought a shaved, modern rug of creamy white, and had the wall opposite the windows partly covered with mirror.

She covered her new upholstered furniture with puffily quilted material, and sent to New York for some big crystal lamps that she had seen advertised.

The night the lamps arrived and her room was complete, she was so excited that she sat on her glasses and broke them. But she could see plenty well enough to catch a cruel glimpse of herself in the mirrored wall. She stared at herself consciously for the first time in years—in her dun-colored dress and flat-heeled shoes she looked like a drab scarecrow in this sophisticated, delicate room.

"I can never let anyone see this room," she thought in complete confusion. "I'd make myself a laughing stock."

But she couldn't bear to change the room—she really loved it. At the end of the week she decided that she couldn't spend the rest of her life scurrying past the mirror. If the room didn't fit her she would fit herself to the room. She spent a harrowing day in a beauty parlor, and then went clothes shopping.

She never did get around to having new glasses made. Her friends all say that this is what caused her to change so for the better, for she looks ten years younger without them. But she knows that this is putting the cart before the horse—if she hadn't copied that beautiful room she would never have broken her glasses in the first place, nor had that first permanent, nor bought that blue suit. Her friends hardly remember what she used to be like—anyhow, they know that she is a sweet, sociable person now. Probably only her mother's Persian cat (who is color-blind, poor thing) could recognize her as that timid woman in a brown dress and horn-rimmed spectacles.

4

WALLS, DOORS AND FIREPLACES
How to Make Them Count

Now that we're ready to dive into the details, let's begin with the big ones. Walls, doors and fireplaces are actually part of the shell of your room. Yet they are also decorative details, and count in the same manner as a large piece of furniture. They will be a strong factor in your final effect.

Walls

There are so many effective methods for decorating your walls today that it's hard to know where to begin. A few years ago wallpaper was practically the rule. Then, more recently, we tore all the wallpaper down and paint took the lead. Right now wallpaper is charging ahead again. So, although it is really a dead heat between paper and paint, we'll start with the paper.

Wallpaper

The wallpapers today offer an enormous variety of patterns. There are wide, striped papers, figured papers, paper that imitates wood paneling, solid color papers and papers that have beautiful flowered patterns copied from old English or French designs. Washable wallpaper is also available, and is eminently practical.

Marbled wallpaper is smart at the moment. I've seen a very effective combination that blended green and white, another that mixed mustard yellow and gray, and one that used two different tones of white.

A few years ago in Vienna they started the vogue of using wallpaper with the stripes running horizontally around the room. It is most unusual, but personally I don't like it. It makes me feel as though I were in a cage.

Whatever you prefer, select your wallpaper with great care. There's going to be so much of it that you've just got to be cautious. Remember the trick I suggested before—get a good big sample, even if you have to pay for it, and hang it up for a day before you order the lot. Remember, too, that the design is going to repeat itself over and over again. Whether you've chosen stripes, cabbage roses, or one of the particularly lovely Victorian papers sold today your wallpaper carries the room on its back.

Your paper can do a lot toward altering the size or shape of your room. It also gives a room a very furnished feeling—you won't need so many pictures or accessories. A small room sometimes looks smaller if you paper it with a big splashy pattern. A larger room might need that big pattern—a tiny design would look fidgety. A wallpaper band around the top of a high room, right below the ceiling, will make that room seem lower. A highly cheerful effect can be attained by papering the ceiling as well as the walls.

As you select your wallpaper it's a good time to decide about your ceiling. If you don't want to paper it, the ceiling can match the background color of the paper. Or it can match a dominant color in the pattern of the paper. For instance, in a room hung with flowered paper the ceiling might match the pink of the roses or the pale green of their leaves.

Paint

PAINTING YOUR WALLS allows you great freedom in your selection of color. Don't be afraid to use it. Walls today can be painted any color under the sun just as long as it's a fresh, lovely shade.

As a general rule light colors should be applied with a dull finish and dark ones with a very high gloss. By a high gloss I don't mean anything fancy like glazing. The average painter, or inexperienced decorator, loves complicated systems of glazing and placing one shade over another. I think the crisp, fresh note is much to be preferred. Three coats of the same color, applied with a finely stippled finish, will give you the right texture. This stippled finish is particularly useful in an old house where the walls are disfigured or patched. It will conceal disfigurements that a smooth finish would emphasize. If such cracks or bulges are too bad to hide, stretch the walls with canvas or burlap and paint over that.

Dark colors for wall paint are being used much more today than they ever have been before. For some unknown reason men, in particular, seem to like them. If you do decide on fairly dark walls don't be discouraged when you see them alone before your curtains and furniture have entered the picture. And always remember that dark walls must be relieved by bright color in the rest of your scheme. The curtains in a dark-walled room could be pure white, or brilliant Irish green, or flame red, or lemon yellow, or beige, or bright chintz—any light color that would be a definite contrast.

If you want cheap, quick results don't forget the cold- or warm-water paints that you can apply yourself.

If you fancy striped wallpaper and find it too expensive see if your painter can't paint the stripes on your walls. Five inches of color and five inches of pure white gloss will give you the smartest proportions.

Excellent effects can also be obtained by the use of stencil designs on your painted walls. A large lattice might look attractive stenciled on the walls of a sun room, for instance. You can find your own stencil design, if you want, by visiting the public library and looking through books on eighteenth-century or Chinese designs. The library will also have a book on how to copy the design you like—make a stencil of it and use it. Big, rococo moldings can sometimes be stenciled around a large room with excellent decorative effect.

(So many beautiful stunts of this sort cost practically nothing in cold cash—just a little effort and ingenuity. Many of the most successful decorators achieved their success in just this way—not because of imposing college degrees, but because of their personal ingenuity.)

In the average room the cornice should be painted the same color as the walls, *not* the ceiling. This rule, of course, goes into reverse if you want to reduce the height of a room or if the room is papered, since it is not practical to run paper over the ridges of the cornice. Of course, if you happen to have a cove instead of a cornice you can carry the paper right over it. (A cove is a smooth arch connecting walls and ceiling, instead of the usual, molded cornice.)

You can always be something of an architect with your paint. One trick is to paint the reveals of your windows a different color from the walls. In a brown room, for instance, you could paint them white and thus give depth to the window and an impression of more light.

Or suppose you feel that a room is out of balance because the fireplace and two big windows are on one wall, and only two medium-sized **doors** on the opposite wall. You can add weight to the light side of the room by painting borders of a different color around those doors. If you want, you can increase the effect by having the top of the border go right up to the cornice.

There is a vogue today, which I must confess I don't like very much, of painting different walls of a room in different colors. There is, I think, just one time when this is advantageous. That is, when a room is very small and dark. If the wall that has the windows in it is painted white, or a very light color, regardless of the color of the other three walls, an illusion of more light and space will be created.

Another trick is to use both wallpaper and paint in the same room—hanging just one or two walls with paper and painting the rest. The effectiveness of this depends entirely on the individual room and is a matter of taste. The walls in this treatment would probably, though not necessarily, be painted the color of the background of the paper.

Wallpaper and paint are sometimes combined in still another manner. The walls are paneled and the insides of the panels are hung with pictorial paper—the rest of the wall surface painted. This method is used quite frequently in early American and French rooms.

Walls Hung with Material

THIS METHOD of decorating walls was undoubtedly made in heaven for people who rent their houses and don't want to spend money on something they will have to leave behind them when they move. Papering or painting a wall may be too much for you to do yourself. But if you happen to be the sort who likes odd jobs, or have a handy husband, you can certainly hang a room with material.

A one-inch board is nailed around the top of the room just below the cornice. Then the material selected is nailed to that board in gathers or pleats, unless it happens to be canvas in which case it is just eased on.

You can choose any material at all for such hangings—chintz, brocade, canvas, organdy, gingham. When you shop for material don't let the stores keep you in the upholstery department. Dress goods can be used just as well, and are often much less expensive. This is very important since you're going to need a whale of a lot of material. For a room where the material is only slightly gathered, or eased onto the walls, you will need 25 percent more than the actual measurements of your room. If you are going to gather it, or have French or box pleats, you will need 100 percent more than your room measurements—just twice its size.

I saw a beautiful room recently that was hung with polka-dotted organdy. And I designed one myself that was hung with ordinary canvas on which a bold design of roses was stenciled.

All the hints that apply to the selection of wallpaper or paint go for material too. Look and look and look before you leap on any particular selection. If you select a patterned material, remember that you will have a lot of that pattern around, and use solid colors in the rest of your room.

Paneled Rooms

ROOMS PANELED IN WOOD are, to my mind, the most beautiful homelike places imaginable. But I'm not going to pretend to tell you all about them in detail in just a few pages. They deserve a whole book to themselves. If you are seriously interested in a paneled room the best thing to do is to go right to the library and do some research of your own. They are extremely expensive and deserve really serious architectural consideration.

After you do know what you want, go to an architect whose work you know is good—not just any old architect. If such a person doesn't happen to live in your own city write to one whose work you have admired in magazines or books. He will give you the expert advice you need. You can send him the size of your room and its openings, and he can draw up the paneling design to be carried out by your own contractors.

If you love paneled walls, and can't afford the real methods, there are several things you can do about it that you may like just as well.

A room can be sheathed, for instance, with thin boards of knotty pine. Any carpenter can do this for you and it is not very expensive. After the wood is rubbed and polished it will give you almost the same lovely background as a more expensive job. You can also use Flexwood—a very thin veneer, applied like paper.

Or (and this costs even less) take a look at the wallpapers now being made that imitate wood paneling. Some of them are surprisingly realistic and cost very little.

Walls Covered with Cork or Leatherette

CORK IS BEING USED quite a lot as a wall covering. It is very modern in effect, but inclined to run into a lot of money. Frankly, cork walls usually give me the feeling of a business office—but this is just a personal reaction. If combined with bright red or green leather chairs it can be made to look rather like the ultramodern version of a wood-paneled room. It looks well either left its natural color, or waxed to a darker tone.

Leatherette can also be used on walls. This, too, gives a room a lived-in quality—gives the same impression of permanence that a panelel wood wall does.

I know of one particularly handsome room (a man's) done in

leatherette. The main color scheme was green and red. The leatherette on the walls was red, with white molding and a white chair rail. The dado (space between chair rail and floor) was painted a dark bottle green. Sporting prints, mounted on wide white mats and framed in dark green, contrasted well with the sealing-wax red walls. Old mahogany furniture was used, and old English chintz for curtains.

Altogether, we have five ways in which we can treat our walls: Wallpaper, Paint, Hung with Material, Wood paneling, or sheathed in such unusual materials as Cork or Leatherette.

The next thing that concerns us is what breaks up those walls—our doors.

Doors

DOORS ARE USUALLY ORPHANS—nobody pays any attention to them. Actually they can contribute a great deal to your whole decorative scheme. Naturally, if your room has too many doors, or you don't like their looks, you will want to make them as inconspicuous as possible. In this case, paint them to match the walls. Or cover one up with a screen that hides the whole door, trim and all. But if there aren't too many, and they are fairly good-looking, plan to make use of them.

(Notice the sketch which shows five different methods of decorating the *same* door.)

The color of a door, and the way in which it is distributed, can turn your doors into ornaments instead of just blank spaces in the wall. You may want to paint the whole door a different color than the walls. In a beige room with green curtains, for instance, you might paint the doors green.

Ornaments can be used to excellent effect on doors. Just because they have to swing doesn't mean they can't have something fastened firmly on them.

Glass doors always irritate me. They don't do what doors are born to do—give you privacy. They are really only an asset if they lead out-of-doors and thus offer you a view. Within the house have them exchanged for real doors if you can, as they are definitely old-fashioned. If you can't change the entire door, the glass can be covered with plywood. (Not a big carpentering job.) The glass can also be painted to match your walls or trim.

Whatever you do to your doors, don't just forget them. They are full of possibilities.

Fireplaces

I DON'T BELIEVE anything in clever decoration can do as much for a room as a glowing fire in an attractive fireplace. As soon as there is a fireplace in a room the whole room centers around it. Men and dogs love an open fire—and they show good sense. It is the heart of any room and should be kindled on the slightest provocation. I never can understand people who have perfectly good fireplaces and never light the fire even when expense is no consideration.

Personally, I feel that to have a mantelpiece in any room is such an important decorative feature that I would rather have a fire of imitation gas or electric coals than none at all. Today there are numerous fireplaces sold that are cleverly designed to imitate coal or log fires. The gas coals, which are installed in a hob grate, are unbelievably realistic. Real flames curl up over the specially manufactured coals. They require, of course, a gas connection and a one-inch pipe, to draw. If there is no way of installing a gas pipe, electric grates are the alternative. These are made with revolving metal fans which give the sensation of dancing flames. If you scatter a dozen pieces of real coal on top of the imitation coals you will be surprised at how convincing it looks. My advice is to buy the mantelpiece you want and then equip it with the most realistic coal equipment you can find. Sometimes a good mantelpiece will have a poor fire in it, and vice versa.

There are imitation logs as well as coals. Those that I have seen, however, are not as realistic as the coals.

If you have a definite feeling that you don't want an imitation fire of any kind I suggest that you install your mantelpiece and pretend that there is something wrong with the chimney so that you can't light the fire. Then you can set up your big brass andirons and lay a real fire of birch logs, kindling and paper. Then make believe that the chimney just can't be fixed—or that it's always summer in your house—and don't light the fire. Or you can keep your fireplace filled with fresh boughs of pine instead of an imitation fire.

Too many people, even though they have fireplaces and love them, neglect them in their decorative plans. They regard the fireplace as part of the structure of the room about which they can do nothing. Don't make that mistake. Think of your mantelpiece as a piece of furniture— and just about the most important piece in the room.

If you have a fireplace that is just plain ugly do consider having it altered or have a whole new mantel put in. It doesn't cost as much as you'd expect and often changes the whole appearance of the room. (On the following page are sketches of different types of mantelpieces I have found satisfactory.)

If your fireplace is bearable but not particularly good you can make it

fade into the background of the room by having it painted the same color as the walls. It can also be improved by painting the facing and inside. A shiny black facing looks well and is practical. Or you can have it all white as the English do. (Don't forget the inside—that should be painted too.) Don't leave it just plain brick unless it is a log cabin sort of room. Black or white marble facings are equally effective, and black slate is also good. Delft tiles suit certain Colonial rooms, and mirror is sometimes used also.

If you have a handsome mantelpiece and want to call attention to it, you can do so by the way you paint it. A fireplace with columns on each side, for instance, might be painted black and the columns painted white. The whole thing could be marbled. Or it could be bleached down to the natural wood. I know of one very effective fireplace (the type that has no mantelpiece but is just a frame of wide bolection mold) where the facing is covered with leatherette. Some have chromium facings, too, and I've seen one where not only the facing but the whole mantelpiece was made of glass. On the whole, it is smart today to be different in the way in which you handle your fireplace.

A common mistake in many fireplaces is to have the actual over-all dimensions of the whole thing too big for the room and the decorative detail too dainty. The columns on either side are often too delicate, the scrollwork too small. (The sketch on the following page illustrates right and wrong proportion.)

Your fire tongs, andirons and fender should all be sturdy and large, too. Nothing looks sillier than a big fireplace with dinky little andirons that look as if they couldn't possibly bear the load of the logs.

It is best to keep your andirons simple as well as large. I saw a set that were made of three large glass balls that were very effective. But you

WRONG   RIGHT

are liable to grow tired of them if they are too cute—cats, owls, dogs and so forth. Personally, I prefer brass or chromium to anything else. They mirror the flames so much more cheerfully. If you do have brass andirons and fender be sure to keep them gleaming. No fireplace is attractive unless it is spick-and-span and ready to use.

Now that you have a fireplace you like and a mantel you like, the next step follows as the night the day—you want to put something on the mantel and something over it.

The same mistake that is so often made in the size of the decorations on the fireplace itself is repeated in the size of the ornaments placed on the mantel. They are almost always too small. A mantel is a place for something really decorative. It is not the place for something so small and exquisite that it must be held in the hand to be appreciated. If you have some beautiful small ornaments that you long to display place them on a table—not on the mantel. Two big vases from the five-and-ten-cent store will give a more decorative effect if they are the proper size and shape. A good rule is to double the size you think you need when you go shopping! You won't be far wrong.

When you select those mantel decorations try to follow the general line of the fireplace itself. If it has columns, follow them on up with bottles or vases placed above them.

Above everything, don't litter your mantelpiece with too many odds and ends. Nothing gives a room a messy appearance any faster than a mantelpiece that carries so many objects that it looks like a curio shop.

When you hang something over your fireplace try again to follow the general line of the fireplace itself. You may find that a tall narrow picture looks much better than a big square one because it matches the proportions of the whole structure more accurately.

You can be original in what goes over your mantel too. The blue room, pictured on page 32, used a collection of decorative china to excellent effect. You may want to cover the wall over the fireplace with a great sheet of mirror stretching right to the ceiling. A picture can be hung right on the mirror, if you want one.

Whatever care and loving kindness you lavish on your fireplace will be repaid, I know, a thousand times. It is one of the most grateful and comforting spots in your house—the spot that bred the old superstition that a cricket on a well-brushed hearth meant a happy home.

CASE HISTORY OF A YOUNG LADY WHO WAS
TAKEN BY SURPRISE

Miss Ash had spent an exciting week. She had moved into an apartment that had countless possibilities and had started to decorate it to suit herself. And she had met Mr Rice—a young man who impressed her as she had never been impressed. Naturally, she wanted to impress him right back.

When he telephoned and asked her to dine with him the very day after she had met him she was thrilled and frantic at the same time. Her apartment wasn't nearly finished. Being instinctively distrustful of man's imagination when confronted by something incomplete she was sure he wouldn't realize that she was the most stupendous homemaker he had ever known. And she had foolishly told him to call for her at her home and have a glass of sherry before dinner.

She looked around her living room in a fighting mood. After all, that was the only room he would see and perhaps she could think up a trick or two. The walls had been finished—they were painted a pale, soft green. She had had the panels of the good old mahogany doors freshly waxed and had the trim painted white. Her fireplace was the room's chief pride. It had lovely lines and was of black marble. She had painted the inside bricks white and by great good luck her big brass andirons and fender were already installed and shining.

But her curtains weren't up—her rug wasn't down—her furniture was sadly lacking its new upholstery. Still she wouldn't give up. In her mind's eye the room looked beautiful. Finally, she got an inspiration.

She dragged her sofa over in front of the fireplace and threw yards of the chintz she had selected loosely over it. Then she rushed out to do a little shopping. When she came back she placed the dogwood she had bought in big glass vases at each end of the mantelpiece. She arranged a coffee table with a huge glass ash tray, matches, cigarettes, sherry decanter and glasses beside it. Then she turned out all the lights and placed loads of candles all around the room in five-and-ten-cent store glass holders (purchased on that same hurried shopping trip). The candlelight was so much softer than ordinary electric light that it threw the corners of the room into melting black shadows.

When Mr Rice came in he was plumped down on a comfortable sofa before a great crackling fire. And such is the almost hypnotic effect of jumping flames, soft lights and a beautiful background color, that it is doubtful if he ever noticed that there were no curtains. He just got the main impression—he was in the shell of a lovely room and sensed it.

That was two years ago. Now no one can tell him anything about decorating or good housekeeping. He claims his wife knows it all.

5

FLOOR COVERINGS AND CURTAINS

Rob Peter to Pay Paul

IN THE LAST CHAPTER we talked about walls. Once you've done that you find yourself thinking about your floors almost simultaneously—it's only natural to plan the two biggest areas in your room right on each other's heels.

Just as in the case of walls, there are many ways of treating floors and their coverings today. We use carpeting, rugs, linoleum, cork, rubber tiling, brick, marble, zenitherm—even glass. Even if you just stick to wood floors you can have them of oak, pine, walnut, ebony or teak!

If you plan to install a hardwood floor by all means consult an expert. Just as in the case of paneled walls I'm not going to pretend to tell you all about a specialist's subject in a few paragraphs. The same thing holds true of a marble floor—it is a big, expensive job and requires the advice of a designer.

But even if you already have good wood floors, you probably will use rugs or carpeting of some sort on them. And that I can talk about in a way that I hope will help you without slighting the subject.

Rugs or Carpeting

ALLOVER CARPETING, from one wall to the other, has taken a new lease on life now that weaves with invisible seams have been invented. This type of carpeting does give a room a rich look. And it definitely makes a small room seem larger. It is also very useful in a room of irregular shape. It does entail a certain amount of unkeep, however. Cleaning is much more difficult—you really have to go into the corners with a hatpin. And an expert must take it up, clean it and relay it at regular intervals. Frequently it's worth it, though, for the spacious look it gives a room. There is a trend today to go through a whole house or apartment and carpet all the rooms in the same material. This unity of plan increases still further that feeling of space and quiet, especially in a small apartment.

A room-sized rug of similar carpeting is often more practical and less expensive. Be sure such a carpet is big enough. It should leave about a foot of floor exposed around the edges in the average room—a little more in a large room. And it doesn't have to be square or oblong. Oval, round or octagonal rugs can be used, depending on the shape of your room. You can add a smart touch by using a heavy, three-inch wool or cotton fringe on your rug. The fringe can match or contrast your rug—just as you please. If you use several small rugs, instead of one large one, be sure they are placed in line with the walls—not catty-cornered.

This type of carpet can be bought by the yard in very beautiful shades today. I don't think you will have any trouble finding just the color for your particular color plan.

Then there are beautiful, hand-tufted modern rugs. These stick mostly to beiges, grays and off-whites. Some of them introduce design in another color, while others are shaved or sculptured so that they have a pattern of form rather than color.

Many people prefer plain rugs in their rooms—they leave you more free to do as you please with what goes *on* the rugs. A dramatic, colorful, patterned floor limits your use of pattern in the furniture coverings of the room.

For this reason Oriental rugs are not as popular as they were some years ago. They are too difficult to blend with the rest of your colors. A brilliant Oriental rug immediately becomes the most eye-compelling thing in your whole room. Because of this I know quite a few women who have had their Oriental rugs bleached out to pale, dim colors. It sounds sacrilegious, I know, but the softly faded colors that result are very lovely and harmonize with anything.

In addition to Orientals there are, of course, the beautiful old classic rugs—Aubusson and Savonnerie from France, needlepoint largely from England, tufted eighteenth-century carpets, Bessarabian, Chinese, Samarkand—and the best of our own early American hooked rugs. As no two of these are ever alike the only way to judge them is not by name but by whether you honestly like them enough to pay their price.

And that brings us to something about which I feel very strongly. Don't pay too much for your rugs or carpets unless you really have money to burn. So many people have swallowed the salesman's line whole —and believe that you must spend a young fortune on your floor or you'll live to regret it. If you follow their advice I think you are more likely to live to grow tired of it.

Personally, I belong to the group of people who like to look up rather than down, and would much rather be extravagant about the objects I put *on* my rugs than the rugs themselves. Certainly if you have a limited budget (and, after all, the biggest budget in the world still has its limits), don't hesitate to rob Peter to pay Paul—save on your floor coverings so that you can spend cheerfully on other things.

I don't mean that you should buy a cheap, shoddy carpet that won't wear at all—that would be poor economy. Stick to the medium-priced, reputable brands and you'll be all right. But don't be brokenhearted if you're not rich enough to invest in an authentic Aubusson or Bessarabian —you can't go wrong with good, plain carpeting of the color you want. (Certain Aubusson reproductions are fairly good, and many modern hooked and braided rugs are excellent. As far as the other reproductions go, I almost think you're better off without them.) The average attractive room today depends largely on an expanse of plain, lovely color on the floor—or on well-kept, dark floors with small rugs carefully placed.

On the other hand, if you become really interested in the question of antique rugs, their history, weaves, designs and so forth, by all means take up the study seriously. Get books from the library, visit the nearest museum and then go to the dealer in your city who carries antique rugs and get him to show you the different varieties. Don't have any hesitation about doing this—he will love it. Tradespeople almost always enjoy talking about their subject to an intelligent person.

And if you do decide to buy an antique rug remember that even though the rug may be priceless this doesn't mean that it is going to give you the best possible decorative effect. When you buy your rug be sure to keep in mind the entire color scheme of your room.

Fur rugs are being used extensively in more modern interiors, and many people get a lovely feeling of warmth and luxury from them. Don't be afraid of them—they aren't nearly as expensive as they look. I bought some white fur rugs that measured 3 by 6 feet for only $6.00 each. If you want a large rug it is sometimes a saving to buy two or three small ones and have them sewn together. The larger skins are harder to trap and therefore expensive.

You can be original in your rugs, too, if you are planning an original house or room. I saw a log cabin last year that had oblong cowhide rugs in the living room. They were edged with brown leather, and were both appropriate and attractive.

If you have good wood floors be sure to stain them dark brown and keep them waxed. But if your floors are old, soft wood, a good coat of paint will do wonders for them. Dark brown or black paint (high gloss) will always look well, though you can use other lighter colors if you want to. Or, if you are sticking to an early American style, you can spatter your painted floors. This is the sort of job that is real fun to do. Just dip your brush in the paint you want to use for the contrasting scattered dots and strike it sharply with a stick or hammer. It will fly all over the floor in just the hit-or-miss style you want. (Overalls strongly recommended.)

Whatever sort of wood floors you have, keep them waxed and polished within an inch of their lives. The English understand this trick of taking immaculate care of household things. Their floors gleam, their curtains are crisp and white. They spend their money on keeping up old things—and achieve a truly mellow, homelike effect. It doesn't matter so much that things are old or faded if they are beautifully groomed.

Floors of Unusual Materials: Cork, Marble, Glass, Rubber Tiling

THE MORE UNUSUAL MATERIALS are, as a rule, more expensive. Cork floors are very handsome, and ideal for nursery or game room. But their cost should be estimated carefully in advance—it may be more than they are worth to you.

This same warning holds true of marble, zenitherm or the more expensive woods. One of the loveliest floors I've ever seen was made of black ebony and light pearwood. Another was of black ebony and steel. If you feel extravagant and want a dramatic floor, by all means look into these rich materials. You will have them forever, and their care is just the same as the less expensive floor coverings.

Rubber tiling is one substance in particular that may interest you. It isn't nearly as expensive as the others and, if well designed, makes a most unusual and beautiful floor. It can be laid in any design you select, and should be washed and polished just like marble.

Linoleum

LINOLEUM is another substance that is so practical that the designers have really been forced to produce it in beautiful colors and designs. It is the least expensive of all. Of course it doesn't wear as well as rubber tiling, but it wears plenty long enough. You can make up your own simple pattern if you want to, but those available are varied and many are really lovely. In bathroom, laundry, kitchen, nursery, entrance hall or game room, a handsome linoleum floor is sometimes the most comfortable thing you can have, just because you don't have to worry about it.

Tile or Brick Floors

NOTHING IS MORE CHEERFUL than a red tile floor in a French provincial house or a cottage. Brick floors are equally charming in the country. They should be kept highly polished just like any other floor. And since they have a definite cottagey look they need rough textured rugs or straw or hooked rugs on them.

No matter what sort of floors you have, if you place rugs upon them you will find that you'll be happier with rug cushions. Your rugs will wear better too. These cushions are made either of thin rubber or animal hair and are worth the small amount of money they cost. They will keep your big carpets from wearing out too soon. And they will keep you from breaking your neck skidding on the small rugs. If you do that, you will get a fine view of the curtains as you sit down—but you won't appreciate it. (I really mean this warning kindly, even though I did bring it up just to introduce the subject of curtains—because I want to talk about them next.)

Curtains

WINDOWS are the eyes of our house. If we remember that, we won't be likely to make the usual mistakes in their decoration. For the commonest error is to put blinders on our windows—so many curtains and shades that we can't see out or in.

The whole modern tendency is to undress both ourselves and our windows. Glass curtains (and that doesn't mean that they have to be flat against the glass), overcurtains on either side and a shade or blind of some sort, is plenty of clothing for any window. Many people even dispense with the glass curtains and get beautiful effects with just Venetian blinds and overcurtains. You'll be all right if you just refuse to swaddle your windows in so many curtains that they look choked.

This doesn't mean that you should skimp on material. Curtains should always be full, no matter what material you use. Nothing looks quite so forlorn as inadequate curtains that hang limp and skinny as dishcloths. If you are using an inexpensive material be doubly sure that you buy plenty of it. In fact I know, after years of experience, that you will get better effects with yards and yards of cheap material than with one expensive width which you have to split lengthwise. A wide window, for instance, almost always calls for two full widths of fifty-inch material.

Overcurtains

OVERCURTAINS (miscalled "drapes") should usually fall clear to the floor. A room that has the quality of a log cabin or a country cottage may let the curtains stop at the sill, however. And rooms that want to strike a more luxurious note should have curtains that lie on the floor for ten or twelve inches.

The old idea that only certain types of curtains are appropriate for certain types of rooms strikes me as silly. If you are planning a highly stylized room and intend to send to Europe for authentic French fringe, that's a different matter, of course. Then the museum is the place for you to gather your ideas—not this book. For I'm talking about how to create rooms that are beautiful for beauty's sake and not for the sake of a stylized pattern, however lovely.

Your curtains can do things for your room, no matter what type you select. A curtain that hangs straight to the floor will make a room seem higher than one that is looped back. Turn back to Chapter 2 on Backgrounds and refresh your memory on the ways in which curtains can alter the shape of uneven or badly placed windows.

If you choose your color wisely your curtains will provide a rich background for your furniture. And if you use washable glass curtains that can be kept fresh and crisp those curtains will give your windows the appearance of light and air that is the keynote of modern window dressing.

Any of these things is really more important to the average room than that the curtains should be of a certain style. For my own part, I am almost always contented with simple, straight hanging curtains, occasionally trimmed with a wide, bulky fringe. Other people expect something much more elaborate of their curtains—perhaps even those stiff,

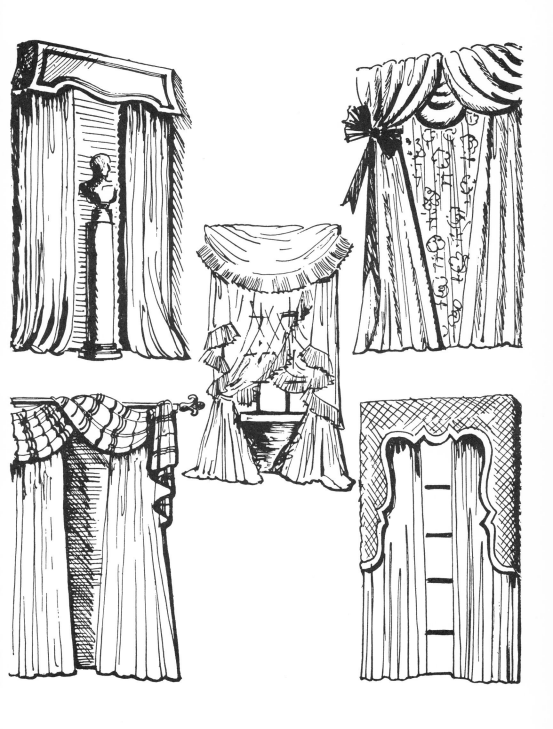

shaped valances that run clear to the floor down each side of the window. (The English call them pelmets.) These can be covered with fabric, wood or leatherette, but they are nothing for an amateur to tackle—call in an expert upholsterer.

Not all curtains need lining, especially if you get plenty of material. Most of them, I'll admit, hang better and last longer when they are lined. But if you don't feel like lining them this is an economy you can make with comparative safety as long as you are generous with material.

If you decide to line your curtains, very beautiful effects can be obtained by lining them with a different material. Rough white brocade curtains could be lined with coral-pink satin, or chintz curtains could be lined with red, or solid red lined with chintz. The English use this last combination a lot (a solid color lined with chintz), and it looks particularly lovely from outside. A dark green curtain might be lined with bright lemon yellow with beautiful results.

So many curtains are just dull. Don't let yours be!

Glass Curtains

YOUR UNDERCURTAINS, or glass curtains, should be of some thin crisp material, whether you place them over Venetian blinds or plain white window shades. Fresh book muslin is practically a classic here. Just as a well-tailored Scotch tweed suit is in style for years, so white muslin glass curtains are always fashionable. You may have to let the hem of your suit up or down, but you won't have to worry about your muslin curtains at all. But do be generous here with your material as well as in your overcurtains. If you exaggerate the ruffles—make them eight inches wide and fluted—you will heighten the look of freshness. You will also increase your laundry problem a little bit but it's worth it.

Blinds

IF YOU DON'T WANT to bother with glass curtains at all you can do wonders with Venetian blinds. They are much less expensive now than they used to be. Personally, I prefer them white with white tapes but you can get them in lovely colors. And by planning the color of the blinds to match or contrast with your walls you can make them a real part of your decorative scheme.

Bamboo blinds are also available now and are even less expensive than Venetian blinds. But since they don't tilt they aren't as practical for controlling light and air. They look lovely left in their natural color in a pine room, though they can be painted to match any wall. If you happen to have very deep window reveals, inside shutters can be charming.

But whatever you select for your windows, remember all the things we've discovered about planning a color scheme as a whole. Gather all your samples together when you go curtain shopping—wallpaper, the shade of the ceiling, upholstery fabric, rug sample. That's what I do myself to be sure I am making a wise selection—and I design hundreds of rooms every year. Then when you've found some material you think is right bring home a good big sample and pin it up. No matter how highly trained your color memory becomes it never pays to ask too much of it.

CASE HISTORY OF A LADY WHO GAVE SOMETHING TO HER MOTHER-IN-LAW

Mrs Quince didn't like her living room. She looked at it crossly one rainy morning and made up her mind on that point once and for all. She also felt helpless about it. She owned a really valuable Oriental rug—a beautiful thing that fairly glowed with color. That was just the trouble, and Mrs Quince knew it. The rug glowed. Her room did not. And if she tried, as she had several times, to introduce a livelier note in curtains or chairs, the rug stood right up on its brilliant hind legs and screamed at the new colors. Mrs Quince read somewhere about having Oriental rugs bleached and timidly mentioned it to Mr Quince.

"What? Bleach a priceless Oriental?" he gasped. "Great-aunt Susan would turn in her grave if she knew you had bleached her favorite rug." The Quinces were all strong-minded people, and so Mrs Quince, who had only married one and who was a gentle soul, certainly didn't want Great-aunt Susan to turn in her grave. She just brooded. Then one day she solved it. In a burst of generosity she took her mother-in-law out to tea and told her that she really felt that Aunt Susan's rug belonged in the family home after all. She sent it there the very next day and the older Mrs Quince is tickled to death both with it and with her generous daughter-in-law. Young Mrs Quince is happy as a grig. She has done her whole living room over, from top to toe, and the first thing she bought was a shaved modern rug of pale beige. It has to be cleaned three times a year, but she doesn't care.

6

UPHOLSTERED FURNITURE
What Slip Covers Can Do for You

If you are the average smart woman who has never made a study of furniture and its arrangement you're like a man who has an undiscovered oil well on his property. This is especially true of your upholstered pieces. What they are, and the manner in which you group them, can change the whole appearance of your room.

Upholstered or overstuffed furniture has become increasingly popular in recent years. There are several perfectly sensible reasons for this:

1. Upholstered furniture is much more comfortable.
2. Its bulk sits solidly on the floor and gives a feeling of security and permanence.
3. Its bulk also gives opportunity for effective blocks of color and design. You can achieve almost architectural results with your large, upholstered pieces.

Comfort

Test your chairs and sofas for comfort first of all. And don't be fooled into thinking that any upholstered piece of furniture is comfortable. The

73

angle of the back is very important—so is the depth of the seat. Sit in any chair a good five minutes before you buy it. And, if possible, take your husband right along with you and fit him to his chair. The most expensive chairs and sofas are not necessarily the most comfortable for you.

It doesn't pay, however, to economize too stringently on upholstered furniture. The very cheapest pieces won't stand up. Their backs will hollow out just behind your shoulders, the cushions will become lumpy, their springs will break. A chair almost always needs a detachable cushion of good down to be really comfortable. The best plan is to buy from a dealer whom you know you can trust. This is simpler than trying to learn for yourself all the technical details about good construction that he has taken years to master. If he is reputable he won't cheat you.

So much for comfort. The fact that upholstered furniture is bulky enough to give you the sense of security I mentioned before, and also to give you an opportunity to use effective masses of color, means that you must plan its arrangement very carefully indeed.

Balance

A ROOM that is weighted down at one end by a great, heavy sofa that is not balanced by similar weight at the other end is an uneasy room. It gives much the same effect as a ship's deck that is heeled way over with one side much higher than the other. Walking on the sloping deck is uncomfortable and insecure. A badly balanced room will give you the same feeling even though you aren't conscious of it. The fact that you have to adjust, and keep on adjusting, your sense of balance is a continued strain.

Naturally your furniture isn't all going to come in pairs so that you can always match one sofa with another of equal size. It would be dull if it did. But you can get a sense of balance from the clever use of color. Dark colors seem to weigh more than light colors. Your pair of chairs, darker than the sofa, may balance it perfectly. Your big wing chair with a squat little table beside it may hold down that corner of the room just as long as it is covered in a color that will add to its weight. Solid colors will usually make things seem larger and bulkier than they are. And bold, allover patterns will reduce their size because they break up the lines just as army camouflaging does.

Another thing that adds immensely to the restful quality of any room is symmetry. This carries balance a step further. Pairs of things will give you symmetry—twin tables on each side of the fireplace, twin lamps on the tables, twin ornaments on the mantelpiece. Of course you don't want to carry this "twin" idea too far or you will get a stiff, formal effect. But a moderate amount of it is always good. It is best, for instance, to buy chairs in pairs if you possibly can. You will find that two chairs exactly alike will simplify your arrangements beautifully.

Balance and symmetry should always be combined with a free-and-easy atmosphere. A beautiful tree is symmetrical in general outline, but there are no two branches exactly alike. So within the frame of balancing objects your furniture should be grouped naturally, for practical use and a sense of intimacy. You may want to place a sofa opposite the fireplace, with two chairs "talking to it." Or, if you have a very large room, you can place twin sofas on either side of the fireplace and at right angles to it. (Never place sofas catty-cornered—it makes your room look crowded.)

For a room without a fireplace you might want to try a window group. Don't think that you must back the sofa against the window—most of the time you'll just lose the view and get a draught down the back of your neck. Place it at right angles to one side of the window, faced by two chairs with a low table between them. You might mirror the window sill, splurge a bit on particularly lovely curtains, and have a row of potted plants like footlights on the mirrored sill. This sort of group would need something pretty important to balance it on the opposite wall: perhaps a large, break-front bookcase, or the piano. Or, if you haven't a break-front bookcase or a piano, use a large table loaded with magazines and books. Put two big lamps at either end of the table and hang a mirror or picture over it. Then one mass will equal the other, even though they are entirely different shapes.

The Furniture Itself

I SHOULD EXPLAIN right now that when I talk about "upholstered" furniture I don't mean wing or barrel chairs. They present problems of their own and are discussed at the end of the chapter. Now I'm talking about everyday, overstuffed, comfortable chairs and sofas.

My first tip is to keep their lines simple and not too bulky. Modern upholstered chairs are made with fairly low backs—the old-fashioned, high-backed chairs chopped up the room too much. If you like a chair with a back that is high enough to rest your head against, it can be made with shorter underpinnings so that the actual seat will be nearer the floor. If you have any old upholstered chairs with high legs be brave and have them all cut down. A big, upholstered chair looks so top heavy if it stands up on thin, high legs.

Upholstery Material

WHEN you select the material for your chairs do it with your whole color scheme in mind. Even if you plan to use slip covers all the time there is no reason why both you and your color scheme should suffer while they're being cleaned. So even if the under-material is inexpensive select its color with care.

Be sure that the material isn't so heavy and stiff that it will detract from the softness of the cushions. A hard, unyielding weave will actually prevent you from sinking down luxuriously into an otherwise perfectly comfortable chair. The most expensive chairs are covered in the thinnest, softest material available. You can select inexpensive material that is just as soft.

If you don't plan to use slip covers have your chairs upholstered in a slip-cover style—with a ruffle or band around the bottom that just clears the floor. Legs should never be visible under a slip cover. A long-legged, slip-covered chair always looks to me like a very fat woman teetering along on tiny little legs and feet.

Slip Covers

I MAY AS WELL ADMIT right now that I love slip covers. They are so much more practical than upholstery that they give you greater freedom in your selection of color. And they always give a room a friendly, informal, casual aspect that is the new note in decoration.

Everyone used to think that slip covers were makeshift, or just for summer. *Nowadays there is no room too grand for them.* You can spend a fortune on beautiful material or not—just as you please. Then you can put them right in a Renaissance or Louis Seize room.

You can perform miracles with old furniture with slip covers, and you can also effect an appreciable saving by buying new furniture "in muslin" and using slip covers all the time. If you feel flush you can have two sets—one for winter and one for summer. This will give your house interesting variety, for a change of slip covers can make over the whole atmosphere of a place.

Slip covers are not really difficult to make at home. Upholsterers make an awful fuss about them and try to scare you into thinking they are very hard. But in England they have never fallen for this—in large houses the maid usually runs them up for the whole house without thinking twice about it. Of course this is easier for her because the English use very loosely fitted slip covers. American upholsterers believe that a slip cover is no good unless it fits as tightly as a sausage skin. I don't agree with them at all on this point. Their skintight covers make the chairs look as if they were about to burst. I have all slip covers made comfortably loose.

Most department stores carry excellent slip-cover patterns. The women's magazines, too, can supply full information.

One of the most important things about a slip cover is that it just clears the floor. Chintz usually looks best with a wide ruffle at the bottom. A plain band is always suitable also. It's a good notion to have all slip covers made with generous hems so they can be let down after constant washings have shrunk them. (Or you can have the material Sanforized-shrunk beforehand.) Slip covers that can be washed, rather than cleaned, are a joy. You can keep them so fresh and clean that it doesn't matter if they become slightly faded. Faded things have a charm all their own just as long as they are crisply laundered.

Slip-Cover Material

SLIP COVERS can be made of absolutely anything that isn't transparent. You can use stripes, an allover pattern, brocade, chintz, bed ticking, homespun, bath toweling, velveteen or velvet, corduroy, felt, gabardine, heavy uncrushable linen, awning canvas, quilted material.

Quilted material will be a little more expensive than the rest, but it makes a most soft, inviting chair. You can buy flat material that you like and have it quilted. (I think you will get better results this way than if you buy quilted material by the yard. The ready-made quilting is usually too flat and the design of the quilting is too small.) A solid color looks lovely if it is quilted in a very large flower pattern that stands right up puffily from the goods. Or, if you select patterned material, the quilting can outline the pattern.

The main thing is to be open minded in your choice of material. As I've said before, wander in and out of the upholstery department in the stores. You may find what you want in the dress goods department and it will probably be less expensive.

Color

YOU WILL, OF COURSE, select your slip covers with your whole color scheme in mind. All the rules about wallpaper, rugs and curtains apply to slip covers as well. In a matching room you might want your furniture to melt right into the walls, and would match the beige walls with beige slip covers. (My tip here is to get the material first. It is easier for your painter to mix a color to match material than it is for you to find material that exactly matches a finished paint job.) In a contrasting room you might use bright yellow slip covers against dark green walls.

My personal preference is to have all upholstered furniture in one room covered in exactly the same material. Chairs and sofas cover so much territory that they shouldn't have different colors any more than your walls should be painted in different shades. You can get all the contrast you need in your curtains, your wing and barrel chairs, your side and occasional chairs. (Side and occasional chairs are discussed in the next chapter on Wood Furniture.) However, this is—like everything else--a matter of preference.

You can doll up your solid colored or brocade slip covers by the use of fringe. Wide fringe, welted into every seam, will give a luxurious appearance. For instance, a brocade slip cover with a moss-green background could have moss-green silk fringe. Slip covers of wool plaid could have dark green wool fringe. I had some slip covers at one time that were pure white bath toweling welted with white cotton fringe. The chairs looked like great marshmallows—the sofa like a snowdrift! You can also welt the seams with contrasting cords if you want a more tailored effect.

Wing and Barrel Chairs

THESE CHAIRS are such distinct types that they really stand out from the rest of your upholstered furniture. For this reason they usually look better if upholstered in a different material from your slip covers. They look very smart if deeply tufted, back and front. Or you may prefer to have them covered in a handsome brocade with all the seams trimmed with bulky fringe, either cotton or silk. There are all sorts of beautiful upholstery techniques to investigate: tufting, the use of big buttons or gilt nails, cording, and so forth.

Occasional chairs with wooden arms and legs also require different material on the seats and backs. Your side chairs, too, will do more for your room if you cover their seats in a way that will contrast your slip covers. You may have a footstool, also, that you will want to do in needlepoint or the same material as the side chairs. If you have kept all your ordinary upholstered furniture alike, your wing and barrel chairs, occasional and side chairs, and a possible footstool, give you your opportunity for contrast. In a pine-papered room, for instance, you might use green curtains, chintz slip covers and a wing chair upholstered in red leather with brass nails. Then the side chairs could be done in wide green-and-white-striped bed ticking.

Once you've got all your upholstered furniture don't be afraid to shove it around. Get a handyman if you don't want your husband to indulge in the usual complaint that his wife is the world's demon for moving furniture. Or, if perspiring handymen make you just as nervous as complaining husbands, make a graph paper scale drawing of your room as described in Chapter 14, page 214. Then try out different arrangements until you know you have balanced your room as best you can.

Stand in the doorway and look the whole thing over consciously and as if you had never seen it before. Decide whether you've concentrated too much chintz at one end of the room, or whether your chairs silhouette pleasantly against the curtains. And remember all the things you've learned about Color and Balance as you do it.

7

WOOD FURNITURE

Tricks of the Trade

YOUR CURTAINS ARE HUNG, your rug is down, your upholstered furniture is all arranged. What a surprisingly small amount of space is left for wood furniture!

On the whole, upholstered furniture has become so popular that it has almost crowded wood furniture out of the room. On a limited budget I know I should recommend concentrating on the upholstered pieces almost to the exclusion of wood.

There is, however, certain wood furniture which you will really need in the average living room for the sake of comfort as well as charm.

1. One pair of end tables for your sofa.
2. One large, low coffee table.
3. Occasional chairs (at least 2 straight and 2 with wooden arms).
4. Occasional end tables for upholstered chairs.
5. Desk (not a necessity in the living room if you have space for it somewhere else).

There are other things you may want either to suit your individual habits or because you have a very large room.

6. A folding tea table which can be produced when needed.

7. A card or backgammon table.

8. A pair of low tables to go on either side of the fireplace.

9. Screen.

10. Radio.

11. Break-front bookcase.

12. Piano.

13. Large table to carry books and magazines.

All the last things mentioned are matters of individual requirements. The average living room can get along very nicely with just the first five listed.

As soon as you start thinking about wood furniture you are confronted with what used to be a bugaboo—period furniture. It is nothing to be in the least worried about today. The study of period furniture is a fascinating, romantic subject. It takes you right back into the homes and lives of the people of the past. But you don't *have* to know all about the homes of the past in order to furnish your home of the present delightfully and smartly.

When we Americans first took up period furniture we did so with our usual terrifying enthusiasm. It wasn't enough to have one Sheraton or Early American piece in a room—there couldn't be anything else but that one chosen period. Everybody tried to make each room just as museum-like as possible. And those people who didn't feel like plunging into the necessary research work became very nervous about the whole thing.

We've learned now that it's not really comfortable to live in a museum. The spinning wheel that cluttered the living room has been packed off to the attic, as well as the chair no one could sit on and the sideboard that was always too big for the dining room anyhow.

We now deliberately introduce notes that will make a room less formal—more comfortable, more easygoing. That's one reason why slip-covered, upholstered furniture now fits in anywhere at all. We jumble our periods cheerfully—just as long as they harmonize in *size* and *scale*.

This harmonization, however, is something that you should watch with an eagle eye. It is not so difficult to catch incongruities of size. We're not likely to combine fragile little Louis Seize chairs with a massive Spanish table, because it would look just plain silly. But it takes a little thought to see what architects call scale.

The scale of a chair is the detail—the type of arms, legs, carving or ornamention. One chair that has exactly the same over-all dimensions as another may look twice as large and heavy because of its detail. Scramble your periods all you like, but be careful that what you select gets together in a congenial manner with the rest of your furniture.

And again I urge you to buy in pairs if you possibly can. Too many odd pieces, no matter how charming, will give your room a mixed-up appearance.

Another old idea that has been hooted off the stage is that all the furniture in one room must always be exactly the same wood. All mahogany furniture, or all walnut, or all maple, used to be the only combinations considered "correct." Don't hesitate for a minute to combine different woods as long as the general effect is attractive.

Just to be neat about this matter of wood furniture let's take up the different items that you'll probably need as we listed them at the beginning of the chapter.

End Tables for the Sofa

THE END TABLES that flank your sofa are more important than many people realize. They are so often too small and too fragile. They should

LIVING ROOM IN A REMODELED COUNTRY HOUSE
Smart Accessories Rejuvenate an Old Room

THE PROBLEM To create a pleasant, distinguished living room in one of those nondescript, formless houses built about sixty years ago—without making structural changes or spending too much money.

THE SOLUTION 1. The entire background of the room is painted clear watermelon pink—walls and woodwork.

2. The fireplace and mantelpiece are also painted the exact shade of the walls. This was done because their proportions are definitely awkward, but the budget did not permit a real remodeling job, so the next best thing was to fade the whole thing into the walls as much as possible. (It is interesting to know that the fireplace facing was first painted shiny black. Then it became apparent that this made it too conspicuous, and it was painted pink like the walls.)

3. The allowance for curtains was adequate but not extravagant. So they are made of yards and yards of inexpensive white book muslin, rather than a skimpy amount of a more expensive material. Their billowing crispness is delightful when the sun shines through them.

4. The floor is stained very dark, and the rug is of rough, thick white carpeting.

5. The lamps are simple white plaster bases with plain white pleated shades lined with palest pink and trimmed with plain white grosgrain ribbon.

6. The old tables (that hold the lamps) were all ruthlessly cut down to the same comfortable level.

7. The slip covers are of quilted chintz—flowers on a cream background. (Notice that the arms of the old sofa are really too heavy to be graceful, but the allover pattern of the chintz somewhat camouflages their bulk.)

8. The emphasis of the whole room is actually the two big coffee tables before the fire. They were specially designed with the tops of black Carrara glass, the sides and legs covered with dark bottle-green leather. The gleaming black tops act as a deep, inky mirror for anything that is placed on them. (The actual size of the tables is given on page 87.)

9. The large bubble ash trays look particularly smart on the coffee tables, and the Lowestoft bowls of flowers are charmingly reflected in their surface.

be large enough, and sturdy enough, to carry good big lamps. Also, the end tables should be exactly the same height as the arm of the sofa. This last rule is not only for the sake of appearances (though it will help them decidedly) but for comfort. If you have to reach up or down to your table, as you sit on the sofa, it's an awkward nuisance.

I prefer round end tables to square or oblong ones. An oblong table continues the line of the sofa and makes it seem longer, and the average sofa is plenty long enough. A round table at each end breaks the line and turns the whole thing into a group.

Coffee Table

A sofa is robbed of half its comfort unless it has a roomy, sturdy coffee table before it. Why these sofa tables are called "coffee tables" I don't know, for they are used for dozens of things besides serving tea or coffee. Actually, they replace the old-fashioned round table that sat right in the middle of a room with a big lamp on it. They can carry magazines, books, a vase of flowers, ash trays, refreshments. The bigger and more usable your coffee table is, the more livable your whole room will seem.

Coffee tables can be either round or oblong. I lean toward oblong coffee tables myself because they serve the whole length of the sofa instead of just the middle.

The height of your coffee table is another of those small items that means so very much. It should be slightly lower than the seat of the sofa. The wider and longer it is, the better. But if it is higher than the sofa seat it will break up the lines of the sofa, look much larger than it is, and be less convenient. If your room is not too small your coffee table can be as big as 5½ feet by 2½ feet, if it's oblong, and 30 inches in diameter if it's round. A good average height for all coffee tables is 11½ inches. The average coffee table, sold in the stores, is too high, too small and too shaky. A fragile, small one defeats its own purpose.

As long as you will want to get lots of good hard use out of your coffee table it's well worth while to have a stain- and waterproof top. Wood can be specially treated to accomplish this, and so can leather. Glass or mirror will also give you a very practical top. Personally I love a coffee table topped with black Carrara glass. It's not as distracting as mirror, but gleams like some deep, black pool.

Keep the lines of both end tables and coffee table as simple as possible —so many that are manufactured are all fancied up with curlicues. If you can't find one you like, and don't want to have one made, you can often get wonderful results by having the legs cut down on a plain kitchen table and putting a new top of black glass or leather on it.

Occasional Chairs

THE SKETCHES OPPOSITE offer you six different types of side chairs, and six chairs with light wooden arms.

Side chairs are almost always placed against the wall. For this reason the pattern of their backs is important—it will be in silhouette. Also because they will be against the wall the upholstery on the seats (and sometimes the backs) gives you a fine opportunity for telling contrast with your curtains or wall color. That is why I said, in the chapter on Upholstered Furniture, that it is a good idea to do the side chairs in a different material from your slip covers.

You can use chintz on the seats of side chairs if you want to but I think plain material looks better. It can be anything you want—leather or leatherette, bold striped material, felt, velvet or velveteen, satin, taffeta or ordinary kitchen oilcloth. I saw some charming Victorian side chairs

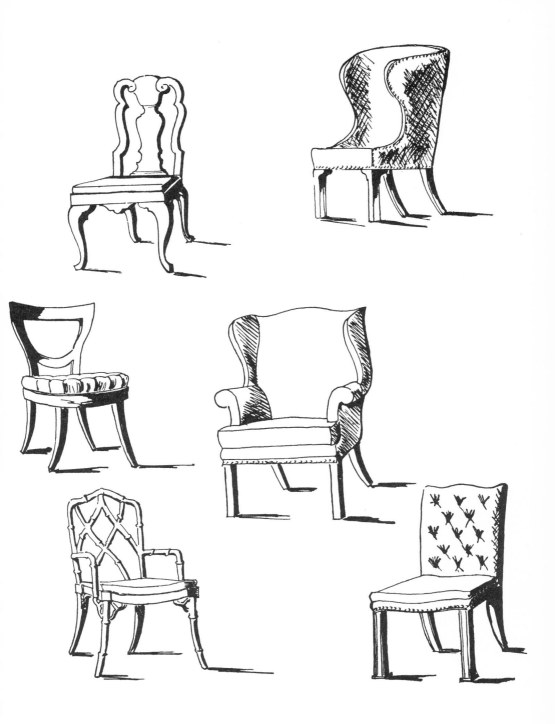

recently that had been upholstered in light blue tufted satin. I have also seen them done most effectively in green oilcloth. Felt makes a very smart, inexpensive covering.

Whatever you select, your side chairs can safely supply bright notes of contrast in your general color scheme.

All the same advice applies to the covering of occasional armchairs. It's usually a good idea to do both arm and side chairs last of all so that you will know just what note of emphasis you want.

Occasional chairs with wooden arms and legs should always be light and easily moved. Their main purpose in life is to be shoved around in your room wherever you need them. And here is the place where a few authentic period pieces will show up to lovely effect. A pair of occasional armchairs that are really something pretty special will give your room just that touch of distinction you want.

Occasional End Tables for Comfortable Chairs

IF IT'S AT ALL POSSIBLE, I think every comfortable armchair deserves its own small table, either beside it or before it. If it goes *beside* the chair it should be exactly the same height as the end tables that flank the sofa. What's more, *every other small table* in the room should be just that same height too. The only exception should be if a table is placed *in front of* an armchair. Then, because it is assuming the same position as a coffee table, it should be exactly the same height as the coffee table. This way all the end tables in the room will be exactly the same height and all the coffee tables will match also.

It doesn't really matter what your occasional tables are like just as long as they are the right height from the floor. The up-and-down effect of a lot of little tables all of varying heights is sometimes enough to bring on an attack of sea-sickness. If you whip out your saw and match the heights of your occasional tables you will do the serenity of your room a big favor.

Desk

A DESK is not a living-room necessity if you have one somewhere else. But many people like one in the living room itself. The first thing to do is to forget the idea that a desk must either be a secretary or something very special in the way of an antique. A workaday, kneehole desk is probably the most comfortable, and it can be ornamental as well. If yours strikes you as ugly, or too plain, try a little face lifting.

You might cover the top with colored leather (say bright green), scrape off all the ornamentation, restain it a dark brown mahogany, and add big, new, brass hardware in place of the old. Or, if you like the old hardware, you may rejuvenate it by having it chromiumed. If the wood isn't good enough to restain you might paint it black with old-gold molding. Or you may scrape the whole thing and bleach the wood. Then you may use a black leather top, or one of cream-colored parchment.

A secretary, of course, is often a beautiful piece of furniture. But it is difficult. It demands a center position on a wall, and so takes up a lot of valuable space. I don't recommend them in smallish living rooms because they really don't do themselves justice if stuffed into a corner. And, after all, seating capacity is what you're usually after in your living room.

You may perk up the appearance of an old secretary if you want to—paint it black outside and red inside and fill it with books or china. Or it may be lined with brocade inside.

Dressing Up Old Furniture

THERE are so many things you can do to transform your old furniture that it really becomes an embarrassment of riches. I mentioned in the

chapter before this that you can work miracles with upholstered furniture by cutting down the high, old-fashioned legs and adding new slip
covers. You can do almost as much for your old wood furniture with a
saw, some paint and a little ingenuity.

Teetering, stork-legged tables make any room seem so full of legs that
it is about to run away. Any tables with such runaway legs will be immensely improved if you cut them down to the height of your sofa end
tables.

A pair of side chairs with backs you don't like can lose those backs
entirely and become a pair of benches for the hall. Or two such chairs
together, with the center legs removed, can make a nice long bench.

A table that is too long-legged and cannot be cut down can be made
to look right if you slip an upholstered bench underneath it to give it
added bulk.

A round table for which there seems no place can sometimes be cut in
two and turned into a pair of consoles to stand against the wall on either
side of the door.

A heavy old secretary can be lightened immensely by removing the
solid panels and replacing them with wire or wooden Chippendale grills.
Sometimes you can get just the note of contrast you've been looking for
by painting the inside of such a piece so that it will show up brightly
through the grill.

Old chairs that seem nondescript can be transformed by a coat of
black paint, with the carving outlined in dull gold. Victorian chairs with
bunches of fruit and flowers at the tops of the backs look charming when
painted white with lettuce-green fruit and given green-and-white-
striped upholstered seats.

Cheap, rush-seated kitchen chairs can be sprayed white all over, then decorated with bright painted flowers on the backs. They give a cheerful pleasant effect. (Try the five-and-ten-cent store decalcomania flowers if you're no artist.)

If you want to combine some odd pieces with mahogany, paint them dark seal brown with gold trim.

Beds can be painted any color you please. Recently I revamped a heavy old four-poster for a client of mine. I had it painted a dull white all over, and hung it with yards and yards of ruffled muslin with pale-green dots. In its original state it had been so large, and so heavily carved, that it dwarfed any room. All dressed up in white and green it was as enchanting and as dainty as a snowdrop.

You can cover almost anything with leather and turn it into something of the moment. Table tops are the most obvious points of attack, but you can do the same thing for the fronts of chests of drawers, boxes and low chests.

If you have a bulging old sideboard that takes up more room than it earns you can take the whole top and back off, place candlesticks on it and a mirror over it.

You can often carry this dismantling trick still further and actually split things in two. A gigantic old cabinet, for instance, can sometimes be cut right in half. Take the base and give it a new top of mirror, wood or leather. And place the old top on a new, simple, short-legged base. You'll have two good chests instead of one towering behemoth.

Sometimes new hardware will change the whole appearance of a piece of furniture. But I'll go into hardware, in detail, in the chapter on Accessories.

You can do a lot, too, by painting furniture the same color as the walls as I mentioned in the chapter on Color.

No matter what you do, don't just give up if you can't afford a lot of new furniture. And don't throw that old stuff away until you've thought about it. Sometimes you can do better things with it than you can with new. And you'll have all the thrill of creating something yourself!

CASE HISTORY OF A LADY WHO ALWAYS CRIED POOR

Mrs Gentleton is the sort of woman who has seen better days and can't forget it for a minute. Since her husband's death her income has been more than cut in half—and so has her life. She is so obsessed with the idea that she hasn't as much money as she is accustomed to that she doesn't do much but bemoan this fact. As a matter of fact, Mr Gentleton has been dead long enough now so that she should be just as accustomed to her slightly shrunken income as she was to the old, generous one.

But she just won't face it—she folds her hands and spends her whole time longing for everything she can think of that she can't afford. She has grown very lonely, too. It is always embarrassing to listen to anyone talk about financial difficulties, and although her friends would probably stick by her in spite of this she is so ashamed of her straitened circumstances that she entertains very seldom and then most ungraciously. Window-shopping is about her only diversion—she aggravates herself by going to the most expensive shops in town and looking at the most expensive things they carry. Then she comes home and mopes because her own house has grown shabby and dull with the years.

This state of affairs might very well go on forever except that Mrs Gentleton has recently let herself in for something that has proved most astonishing. She became so lonely that she invited her cousin Lucy to come and live with her. Lucy has never been well off and was glad to accept.

But perhaps because Lucy never *has* been well off she is blessed with a rich fund of spirit and imagination.

"Martha," she told her cousin crisply, "what you need is a good dose of sulphur and molasses well mixed with gumption. Do you mind if I just steam ahead and make my room look like a human habitation?"

She tackled the gloomy set of furniture the very next day, armed with a pot of apple-green paint and a pair of rubber gloves. Bed, bureau and straight chairs were sleek and crisply green in just a few days. Mrs Gentleton complained that the smell of paint made her faint, but Lucy just laughed and said it didn't last long.

Next Lucy dragged out the old sewing machine and ran up gay chintz curtains with lots of green leaves. She covered the comfortable chair by the window in the same chintz, disguising the bad proportions of the chair completely by letting the chintz fall clear to the floor. Then she threw away the dirty colored, old lamp shades in the room and bought clear white ones at the local five-and-ten-cent store. A new, pale yellow cover for the comforter at the foot of her bed gave her a nice splash of contrasting color.

After that she ostentatiously entertained her friends right in her bedroom—setting up a tea table by the window and using a polished brass alcohol lamp to heat the water.

"Only cheerful room in the house," she explained to Mrs Gentleton. "Cost me just ten dollars though. If you'd let me get at the living room we could give a buffet dinner—have a woman in to help, you know, for just a dollar or so. There's no limit to what I could do to that room with a quart of white paint and a bolt of striped bed ticking."

Mrs Gentleton is thinking it over. But if I know Cousin Lucy they'll be sending out dinner invitations any day now.

8

LAMPS AND ACCESSORIES
They Make or Break Your Room

Effective lamps and accessories can lift any room right out of mediocrity into something as distinguished and gay as a Paris hat.

The fashion magazines have been harping for years on the tremendous importance of accessories in clothes. They are dead right, and very convincing. The result is that most of us know now that we can take a ten-ninety-five plain black dress and make it look like something very special by wearing one perfectly superb piece of costume jewelry. The very first thing we do to inexpensive clothes is to rip off the cheap trimmings and replace them with the best we can find. We have learned that we can alter the whole effect of a nondescript dress by buying an unusual belt and new buttons.

Yet many of us fail to carry this knowledge into our houses. One of the smartest, best-dressed women I know has a dowdy house. Her living room is ruined by fussy, old-fashioned lamp shades, carelessly mismatched fire tools and a litter of unattractive knickknacks on all the small tables. She has two very skinny, wobbly pottery vases on her mantelpiece. You can't help noticing them the minute you step into the room, and making a mental note that they are an ugly shade of green and force the flowers into tight, ungraceful bunches. There is no use going into any more details. They *are* details—but so unbelievably important.

On the whole, I believe that nothing else will pay you such grateful dividends as money and thought expended on accessories. Here's the place to splurge—here's the place to put that money you saved on your carpet. Here's the place that every cent you spend will really show.

Lamps

OF ALL THE ACCESSORIES in your room the lamps are definitely the *first, foremost and most powerful.* Nothing can do as much or as little for you as your lamps. And I would be happy to place a large bet that the lamps in nine out of ten rooms are too small. A small lamp is useless from both decorative and functional standpoints. It isn't much to see, and it isn't much to see by. (The sketch on page 99 illustrates the vast difference the size of a lamp can make.)

Fifty-eight inches is a good, average height for all living-room lamps to measure from the tops of the shades to the floor. (You get this figure, of course, by adding the height of the table, the height of the base of the lamp and the height of the lamp shade. The lamp in the sketch has a 20-inch base, a 15-inch shade, and stands on a 23-inch table.)

Lamps should not only be fairly high, but they should also have bulk. A thin, tippy lamp is a menace to have around and you'll have trouble finding a shade that won't look too big for the base.

(For the sake of clarity I shall talk about living-room lamps from now on, with just occasional forays into the dining room and bedroom. Most of the advice about lamps is general and fits any room, and whatever particular problems arise in bedroom, bath and dining room I shall take up later on in chapters devoted specifically to those rooms.)

WRONG   -CORRECT-

The average living room will probably need only four main lamps—one at each end of the sofa, the other two at other points in the room where comfort demands them. I feel very strongly that these four main lamps should be *exactly the same height from the floor*. No matter what type of lamps you select the tops of all four shades should be on an even line all the way around the room.

I say "no matter what lamps you select," but actually you will add greatly to the balance and chic of your room if the four lamps are identical. Or, if you don't want to have all four exactly alike, at least have two pairs. Better still, have two pairs of lamps and four matching shades.

Lamp Bases

THE BASES OF LAMPS can be made of all sorts of interesting or amusing things just as long as they are big enough. It's often fun to find big jugs or vases with shapes you like and have them wired. Any electrician can do this for you and the cost is negligible. If you like the shape, but not the color, of your discoveries you can paint them white with dull plaster paint.

Beautiful lamps that combine fine dimensions with a glittering delicacy can be made of old hurricane chimneys. These columns of glass were used in the old days to shield candles from the wind. You can find them today at many of the large department stores, and frequently at country auctions or antique shops. They should be mounted on a chromium or wood base, with a matching rod run up through the center of the glass column. (See lamp in photograph opposite page 32, Chapter 3.)

Here are a few other things from which you can have your own lamps made:

1. Old-fashioned demijohns.
2. Molasses jugs.
3. Big cider jugs used by the chain stores.
4. Plain wood cylinders covered with colored leatherette.
5. Old Victorian vases.
6. Gold Empire urns.
7. Big Chinese vases.
8. Blue and white Canton jars.

Of course there are many other possibilities. The main thing is to keep your eyes open for the unusual and entertaining. Then, whenever you have found something you like, make every effort to buy in pairs.

Lamp Shades

LAMP SHADES are like hats—they go in and out of style. And they are probably one of the few things in your whole house that I believe should be kept in the fashion. Old furniture, softly faded chintz and old silver will give your house a mellow quality. But your lamp shades should be

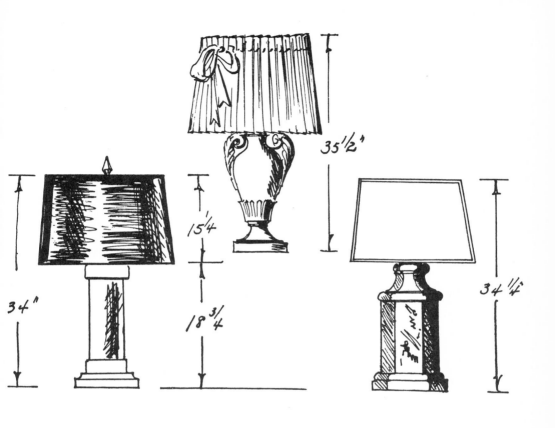

35½"

15¼"

18¾"

34"

34¼"

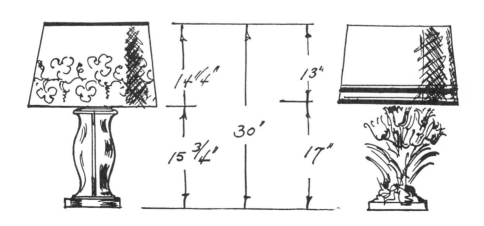

14¼"

13"

30'

15¾"

17"

your modern note. Their styles won't change too rapidly to make this impractical—you probably won't want to change them more often than once every three or four years.

Right now lamp shades are exceedingly simple. They have no more little prints, no more maps, no more dinky ornamentation. Perfectly plain white shades are suitable for any room in the house. Lovely shades can be made of plain white linen, lined with pink if you want a softer light.

Whenever there is any ornamentation on your lamp shades it should fit into your room somehow. Plain white shades could sport a boldly stenciled design in some color that is part of your whole color scheme. I have also seen big drum shades covered in a light chintz that was used elsewhere in the room. I have also seen very handsome shiny brass shades in a dark-walled room, and dark green ones in a pine room.

On the whole, however, most of the modern shades are either of plain white or of some pale color that will give loads of light. The old-fashioned shades of muddy-colored, thick fabrics are rightly unpopular. They weren't pretty, and they made it practically impossible to find your way around.

Be very fussy about fitting just the right shades on your lamps. There can't be any rules about this—it must be decided by the shape of the lamps themselves. But if you squint your eyes and study the combination with the hat comparison in mind, I'm sure you'll find what you want. Watch out for shades that look like big hats on little bodies, or froufrou hats over tailored suits, or little, pinheaded hats on big, fat women.

Lighting in General

THE WHOLE TREND of today is toward plenty of light. It need not be harsh—but let there be light at all costs. This doesn't mean that you have to jam your room with lamps. High-powered fixtures with bulbs that throw light both up and down make it possible to light almost any room more than adequately with just the four main lamps I mentioned before.

You will probably want to supplement them only for special activities—playing cards, sewing, playing the piano. For these things my own inclination is to use a simple, gooseneck lamp, either finished in chromium or painted to fade into the walls. It isn't supposed to be decorative—just functional, and so convenient. Its neck can be craned over fine sewing or over your desk. Two gooseneck lamps give a bridge table the best possible playing light and take up much less room than the clumsy old bridge lamps.

If you have an extremely large room you may have a dark corner that you want to lighten a bit. Here you can resort to inexpensive but effective tricks. One bulb, wired inside a big vase, will cast a soft, lovely glow over the wall. (The vase would naturally be placed on a fairly high piece of furniture so that you couldn't look down inside.) Or two electric bulbs can be placed at either side of your window top, behind the curtains. You can also have footlights installed along the bottom frames of paintings.

I prefer any of these devices to wall brackets in the living room. They may be necessary in the dining room but in the living room I think they do little more than glare in your eyes. There is, of course, an exception to this like everything else—I have used lovely copies of eighteenth-century wall brackets, with real candles in them, in a more formal sort of drawing room, and they supplied a note of real glamour.

Unless you have a particularly beautiful center chandelier I like them even less than I like wall brackets.

If you are fortunate enough to have a garden, or a terrace, by all means play it up with special lighting. A baby spot, attached to the side of the house and trained on the garden or terrace, is the simplest method. Switch it on during summer evenings, or when your garden is beautiful with snow, and keep your curtains parted. Then you can enjoy your garden night and day, indoors or out. And your living room will seem just twice as large.

Coffee-and End-Table Accessories

THE THINGS on your living-room tables should, of course, all be livable things—either things you use or things you love. But remember that they are definitely on display. It pays to splurge a bit on every one of them.

On your coffee table, for instance, you are going to want one or two ash trays. Make them something special—perhaps those huge, bubble glass ones manufactured today. (Bubble ash trays are illustrated in the photograph opposite page 86, Chapter 7.) If you don't feel like spending the five or six dollars apiece that they cost, get two big glass bricks from any large building company. Turn them over, use the hollow in the bottom for ashes, and they will look almost as well.

If your coffee table is large (and I hope it will be), keep flowers on it in a carefully selected vase. Be sure the cigarette box you place there is an attractive one, and always filled. If you keep your eyeglasses case, or a letter opener, on the table be sure they are the most decorative you can find. Place a few magazines (both American and foreign) on one end of the table. This isn't a careless suggestion—I really mean it. Today's magazines give a bright, cheery note that is invaluable. They help conversation along, too.

The tables at each end of the sofa won't have as much room as the coffee table but everything on them should be just as thoughtfully selected. The most important objects they will carry will be the two big, handsome lamps you need there. Then they will probably require plain glass ash trays, but these shouldn't be as large or as unusual as the ones on the coffee table. A few pet books, or any small treasures or mementos you own that are beautiful to look at, belong on the sofa end tables. Even if they aren't beautiful, but have some intimate charm or association for you, put them out where you can enjoy them. A house that banishes all sentiment in a grim pursuit of appearances will only succeed in looking hollow and cold. But make sure that the little objects you place on your tables really *do* mean something to you. Don't allow odd knickknacks to collect just because you never get around to sorting the sheep from the goats.

Vases

A VASE OF FLOWERS or greens will bring even a dull hotel room to life in the most delightful way. The small amount of trouble or expense involved is honestly repaid in real decorative effect. If you find cut flowers too extravagant, stick to the greens. Laurel, rhododendron leaves, huckleberry or pine will all last many days, even weeks.

In the old days vases were almost always highly ornamented and very fancy. Sometimes they were beautiful, at other times they were really too ornate. The modern impulse is to turn those beautiful old vases into lamps, and to keep our flower containers very simple so that they will be unobtrusive settings for the flowers themselves. Clear glass vases accomplish this better than anything else. Select them for size and shape. It isn't in the least necessary to buy the most expensive ones, for when they are full of water and flower stems the quality of the glass itself shows very little. The five-and-ten-cent stores have a fine assortment of small ones. The department stores have the larger ones, with prices ranging from around $5.00. And here, as in chairs and lamps, it is best to buy in pairs.

If you're at all fond of flowers you will probably want some potted plants or stands of bulbs. They can make a room seem cozy and lived in even faster than vases of greens. You will increase their out-of-door garden effect if you leave the pots in their natural color. If you do want to paint them so that they will retain the moisture better for certain thirsty plants, paint them plain white.

And when you place your potted plants in your room do think of them as part of your whole color scheme. So many real flower lovers fuss over their plants patiently and then arrange them with no relation to the rest of the room at all. Notice very consciously that red geraniums look bright and gay on the window sill between your white curtains, or that your potted primrose shows up best on that table near the window where the sun strikes it and makes it glow against the soft blue walls. Plan the best backgrounds, color contrasts and settings for your plants, both in the daytime and at night. Just because your plants must usually live on the window sills during sunny hours doesn't mean that they can't be scattered around your room after nightfall. It isn't enough just to love flowers—you do them an injustice if you don't make the best possible use of their beauty.

Fireplace Accessories

I DISCUSSED fireplace equipment, mantelpieces and their ornaments pretty thoroughly in Chapter 4 so I won't repeat myself here. Just remember to keep your andirons, fender and tongs very large, simple and gleaming. Keep the mantel shelf unlittered and be sure that any ornaments you place at either end are twice the usual size. Your fireplace is the focal point of the room so it should always be in perfect order, just waiting for the match that will kindle the blaze. Little touches like a brightly polished Cape Cod lighter, or a basket of pine cones, will make it seem more friendly.

Hardware

THE KNOCKER on the front door, the doorknobs throughout the house and all the handles and knobs on furniture drawers strike a distinct note in your whole scheme. If you don't own your home you probably won't want to change the doorknobs all through the house. If this is the case, and they are ugly, paint them the same color as the doors. Or, if they are the old-fashioned white china knobs, you can get a charming effect by painting or stenciling bright little flowers on the china. If you do want to change them, I think extra-size brass knobs are the most satisfactory.

A big, shining knocker on your front door will dress it up immensely. It immediately gives an impression of distinction even before the door to your distinctive house has swung open! Unusual, large knockers aren't necessarily expensive either. I picked up a fine eagle knocker in a junk shop last year for just $3.00

New, smart furniture handles can alter the entire appearance of an old and uninteresting piece. They should always be big, simple and shiny. (Unless, of course, you have an authentic antique with dull gold handles.) Take a look at your less impressive chests and bureaus and notice whether they couldn't be completely restyled by new hardware. Or perhaps the old hardware would look entirely different if you had it chromiumed.

Any well-known hardware firm that advertises in the better decorating magazines will send you a catalogue of hardware that will dazzle you with the splendid variety offered. It doesn't have to be elaborate or expensive, either. The simpler, the better—*size is what counts*.

Plain, round, flat knobs of chromium, brass or glass make excellent drawer handles. They can also be something new and amusing—bone, or big wooden spools.

Picture and Mirror Frames

I CERTAINLY shan't presume to tell you what sort of pictures you should have on your walls. That is definitely a matter for your own artistic inclinations to decide. But whatever they are, their framing is a matter that deserves more thought than it usually gets. You can change the whole appearance of many pictures just by the manner in which they are framed.

The old-fashioned frames made much the same mistake that old-fashioned flower vases did. Both vases and frames were often so ornate that they diverted attention from the very things they were supposed to present. A picture frame's reason for being is to set off your picture—not overshadow it. For this reason most modern frames are very simple. Many are of natural wood, completely without ornamentation. Others are painted in one solid color—perhaps white, perhaps some color that will contrast with the walls, perhaps some shade that exactly matches a minor color in the picture itself. A simple bolection mold is the most becoming frame for many pictures.

The desire for plain, unobtrusive frames is so strong today that there is even a vogue for bleaching gold frames. Frames can also be painted the same color as the furniture in the room.

Unless a mirror has a particularly beautiful frame that just suits it, it is often a good idea to give it a new modern frame along with your pictures. Many a fussy old mirror can be turned into a real asset by adding a new, wide frame.

Picture Mats

FRAMES, OF COURSE, are only half the job. The mat that surrounds the picture under the glass is just as important. And most of us are just beginning to realize how much can be done with them.

Until quite recently a two-inch white mat was automatically placed around every picture that was not an oil, no matter what its size. Now we've discovered that much wider mats are often infinitely more effective. Six inches at the bottom of the picture, and four or five at the sides and top, will frequently turn a small picture into something that can dominate a wall. Sometimes the width at the bottom is greatly exaggerated and the picture is actually placed three quarters of the way up the frame.

Mats no longer have to be plain white cardboard either. Beautiful effects may be obtained by using different materials. The color and material used, of course, depend on the picture itself. Here are a few suggestions for interesting mats:

1. Wide white cardboard with a one-inch band of color next to the picture itself.
2. Leatherette—either red or green looks dashing with hunting or sporting prints.
3. Rough textured linen or homespun in cream or beige.
4. Shantung silk in any pale, clear shade.
5. Silver paper—particularly lovely with Chinese or Japanese prints.
6. Marbleized wallpaper—especially good around engravings.

With just a little thought I am sure you can devise beautifully appropriate mats and frames for any pictures you plan to reframe. I feel that every picture, whether it is a masterpiece or a snapshot, deserves the best possible frame. You can, as a matter of fact, glorify the snapshot with a masterpiece of a frame! I had a client once for whom I attempted to do just this, and I must say the results were very successful. My client had a collection of family photographs—no more distinguished or decorative than family photographs usually are. But she cherished them, and although they at first seemed to have no place in her newly decorated bedroom she wanted to keep them where she could see them. So we put identical, plain white frames on all the photographs, and surrounded each with a mat of pale blue shantung silk. The walls of the room where they hung were a soft pink, and the final effect was charming. It combined smartness with some of the owner's own personality. And that, I think, is what your pictures should always do.

How to Hang Pictures

THERE are no specific rules about exactly how high or how low a picture should be hung. It depends entirely on the size of the picture, the height of the wall and the furniture that is grouped against that wall. The only thing to do is test out different combinations until your sense of proportion and balance is satisfied.

There are, however, several principles that will guide you.

1. A picture should always be an integral part of the group of furniture and accessories over which it hangs. (Notice the Right and Wrong sketches—they illustrate this point better than words.)

2. If it is humanly possible, keep the tops of all pictures in a room exactly the same distance from the ceiling. (Don't think this is out of

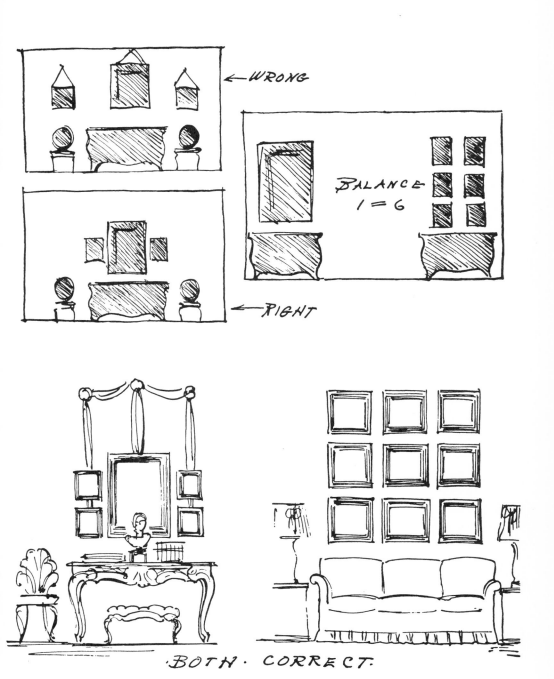

← WRONG

BALANCE
1 = 6

← RIGHT

BOTH · CORRECT.

the question because you have one large picture and a collection of much smaller ones—they can be balanced beautifully by grouping the small ones as illustrated in the sketch.)

Accessories for Serving Food in the Living Room

I SHAN'T DISCUSS dining-room or bedroom accessories in this chapter because they will be taken up in detail in their own chapters. But even in a house with a dining room a certain amount of eating goes on in the living room—tea, cocktails, after-dinner coffee, light refreshments after bridge or the theater. It really all adds up to such a list that I think a folding tea table is almost an essential today. It is so much handier to set it up and then whisk it out of sight afterwards than it is to clear some table of all the things that live on it and then have to put them all back again later. If you don't own a folding tea table and don't want to buy one a bridge table with the legs cut down a bit will do just as well.

If you are already in the habit of serving tea you know what a pleasant, relaxing half hour it gives you. And there is something about sitting behind a lovely tea set that makes every woman feel delicate, romantic and well cared for. Your tea service should match that feeling, and be something really special. Use an exceptionally beautiful tea cloth (put one on your Christmas or birthday list). Get hold of a tea set that you really love—it doesn't matter whether it is old silver inherited from your great-grandmother or luster bought at your local department store as long as it is attractive. You may prefer old-fashioned, sprigged china, or peasant ware accompanied by rough little napkins. You can even use paper napkins as long as they are the nicest you can lay your hands on. (Very pretty ones with your own initials on them can be ordered by mail from the large department stores.) The main thing is to have your tea table as appetizing and as charming as you can make it.

The same thing is true, of course, of serving cocktails or light refreshments. If you serve cocktails frequently one of the less expensive, portable cocktail bars will be a great help. Have a simple good-looking shaker. I myself prefer the inexpensive clear glass ones to the trickier varieties. When you arrange canapés and appetizers try and make them colorful and pretty as well as tasty.

For after-party or after-bridge snacks you can do all sorts of things. You may use jam containers that are unusually bright and cheerful and little jam knives with colored handles. You could get one of those amusing old-fashioned dishes shaped like a hen and fill it with hard-boiled eggs.

All of these suggestions are just the slightest sort of hints. The thing I am trying to convey is to give any food served in the living room a special, party sort of gaiety all its own. You can do it so easily through your choice of accessories.

An Individual Accent

SOMEWHERE among your accessories try to strike one clear, beautiful note that will be the main theme of your whole symphony. One lovely or unusual thing can be the focus of interest for your whole room. And that "accent"—that final touch—often counts for more than a terribly expensive rug or authentic furniture. If you are working on a moderate budget by all means economize on some homely thing and blow yourself to one special accent that really thrills you by its beauty. Your accent can be almost anything just as long as it is unique and eye-compelling.

A Living Room Built around a Screen

I REMEMBER ONE ROOM that grew around a lovely old eighteenth-century Japanese screen. It had a background of tarnished silver and a great bough of blossoms in palest pinks, faded reds and soft cream tones.

The walls of the room were painted die-away green, the floor was dark, highly polished and bare except for a soft white rug before the fireplace. The furniture was most simple and inexpensive, upholstered in faded coral and pale green. The curtains were cream white, with fringe to match. But the first thing you saw when you entered the room was that beautiful screen, mounted flat on the wall above a long, low sofa.

A Room Built around a Set of China

YOUR ACCENT doesn't have to be nearly as imposing as the screen. Another room I know, far simpler than this, began with a set of white china which was willed to a young professional woman of modest means.

The china wasn't just ordinary white, but a sort of luminous, moonlit white. The plates were all square and the knobs on the vegetable dishes were little bunches of fruit. So, around her white china, the owner planned a little country dining room with white walls, white Venetian blinds, white painted chairs and serving table. But she painted the dining table itself real lacquer red. And over the serving table she hung her only other treasure—a big Persian plate of a blue like the sea on a summer day.

Miscellaneous Accents

YOU may own something unusual right this minute that is tucked away in the attic or not played up sufficiently. If you don't, auctions (both country and city), furniture storage warehouse sales, antique shops and decorators' shops are all fine hunting grounds.

There are so many things to look for. Here are just a few suggestions to start you off:

1. A striking modern painting.
2. A beautiful antique hooked rug.

3. A lovely old mirror.

4. A pair of fine candelabra.

5. A length of old French wallpaper.

6. A fragment of Greek sculpture.

7. A piece of intricate needlepoint.

8. A collection of steel engravings.

9. A Chinese ancestor portrait.

10. A red lacquer desk from France.

11. A marquetry desk from Holland.

12. A piece of papier-mâché furniture lovingly inlaid with pearl.

13. Just anything at all—as long as it is out of the ordinary, and lovely.

When you are shopping for an accent, don't be taken in by a sales line. An antique may be as old as the hills and still ugly. Something may have been manufactured yesterday and be rare and beautiful. It may have first seen the light of day in some faraway, exotic country or in the next block from your house. How can that affect it? Trust your own judgment when you buy. Plenty of people have started whole modes by seeing beauty where others passed it by. And plenty of others threw out the very things their grandchildren now collect!

Minor Accents

THERE WILL, OF COURSE, be minor accents in your room too: a particularly handsome pen tray on your desk, a little Staffordshire figure of which you are fond on one end table.

You may want to throw a light decorative rug over one end of the sofa. It might be of white rabbit fur or soft homespun with your initials in the corner, or of green wool or corduroy. Think of your color accent here. And be sure that it's the sort of rug that actually invites you to relax and pull it up over your ankles as you listen to the Sunday Philharmonic concert.

Any minor accent will add immeasurably to the intimacy and charm of your room. It can be as sophisticated or as cozy as you please, just as long as it is distinctive.

On the whole, no accessory is too unimportant to consider. They are the details of decorating, but it is just those details that tone your house either up—or down.

PART II

9

FRONT DOOR, HALL AND LIVING ROOM
As Others See You

This chapter is really devoted to the impression your house makes on the world. Your front door talks about you to everyone who passes by. Your hall and living room gossip about you to all your friends. The combination of the three expresses the hospitality and personality of your whole house.

The welcome that your house extends to guests, to friends, even to your own husband coming home in the evening, should certainly be as cordial as possible.

One of my earliest recollections is of arriving after dark at my grandmother's house in Stockbridge. It was always the same and always thrilling, even when I look back on it after many years. We would clatter up the driveway in my grandmother's old brougham and see the whole household framed in the lighted doorway—my grandmother in her black silk dress, calm but expectant; my aunt, eager and impatient for us to arrive; Ellen, the Swedish maid, beaming in the background; and young Peter (over sixty) waiting to carry our bags upstairs. They were all honestly glad to see us—and they let us know it.

Whenever you go calling, if you are greeted with a smile, if you are not kept waiting a second longer than necessary, if your hostess herself comes to the door, you will get the pleasant impression that you were eagerly expected. Or it can go just the other way. I have one friend who keeps a large, very conscientious watchdog. For some reason I've never understood she doesn't bother to lock him up even when she fully expects company. So the minute the bell rings I stand shivering on the doorstep while the dog barks wildly inside. Then when the door is opened and I step in I must fight the brute off until he recognizes me and is shushed and scolded by his mistress. He is just doing his job, but he makes visiting at that particular house a minor ordeal (at least for the first few minutes).

This personal element, of course, has a great deal to do with the welcome your house extends. If you have servants and don't like going to the door yourself why not ask your servants to open the door with a smile? They will probably like it, and have just been stiff and solemn because they thought that was what you wanted.

Your house, however, can back you up just as effectively as a retinue of old family servants beaming from ear to ear. Some houses seem to say "Come on in" even before the bell is answered. And there are others, in that empty moment before the door is opened, that make you wish you'd never come at all.

Front Doors

THE MESSAGE your front door broadcasts to the world is too frequently overlooked. I think people often go on the theory expressed in the old saw, "My face—I don't mind it for I am behind it." This is a real mistake. Your front door (whether you have a whole house or a small apartment) is the very first impression you have to offer. It is your house's calling card.

Go outside and take a look at your own front door. Is it exactly like the one next door? Is it nondescript? Even a little shabby? If it is, that's a pity, for it's so easy to make it inviting.

If you rent your house you naturally won't want to bother with a new or expensive entrance. But a coat of paint, a pair of potted trees and a big brass knocker will do so much! I once lived in a rented house in Washington that had a most unprepossessing outside. It was a sort of dark, dirty green building on a quiet, rather shabby street. But after I had painted the door the most cheerful yellow I could find, placed big tubs of flowering shrubs at each side of the stoop and hung a huge eagle knocker on the door, my friends told me that they never had to look for the number—they knew that yellow door was mine.

Don't forget the outside of your front windows either—especially those on either side of the front door. Their curtains should look well from the outside as well as inside. Curtains lined with bright chintz are lovely from the street. So are plain white muslin curtains, if they are crossed and looped back to show a pretty potted plant on the sill.

Even if you live in an apartment and your front door is labeled 3-C you can still make it talk your language. I have painted apartment doors to suit myself and the landlords have not minded too much. And you can still use a big, decorative knocker, or hang an ornament on the outside of the door.

Glance back at Chapter 4 where I talked about the decoration of doors and you will find sketches and specific suggestions about their treatment. They can all apply to front doors just as well as the doors within the house.

Halls

THE HALL is probably the one place in your house where you will want to be more or less formal. This doesn't mean that a hall should be so dignified that it is dreary. But because a hall isn't really lived in it is likely to be rather set and tidy. And because it is sparsely furnished balance will be more important than clever accessories.

First of all, be sure there is plenty of light in your hall. You will probably have there one long table or console, and if you place a lamp at each end you will light it much more pleasantly than by using just the ceiling light alone.

Over this long table is often the best place for the good big mirror every hall needs. And on the table you can place a large bowl of laurel or huckleberry. I imagine you are sick and tired of listening to me tell you to place large bowls of greens or flowers all over the house. But I can't help it—they are as much a part of a decorative scheme as beautiful curtains.

Also on the big table you will want a tray of some sort for visiting cards and mail. Since you haven't many other ornaments in your hall make your tray as handsome as possible.

At least one, perhaps two, side chairs should go in the hall since it is occasionally convenient to have someone wait there for a few minutes. A good-looking umbrella stand is a sound investment too. (Try to make it count decoratively.)

The color scheme of your hall floor, walls and ceiling should be considered just as the other rooms in the house were. You may want to match your living-room colors—or you may want to contrast them. Think of your color continuity here especially, since you pass so rapidly from hall to living room.

If possible, have a practical floor in your hall. In the chapter on Floors I mentioned several floorings that are suitable—rubber tiling, linoleum, marble, brick or tiling.

Hall Closets

THE HALL CLOSET is often used for the whole family's heavy coats. Personally, I think it can usually be turned to much better use and coats hung in the bedroom closets with everything else. It is so convenient to have a roomy hall closet to take care of the overflow from the living room. You can store extra folding chairs there, or the folding tea table or bridge table, or the backgammon board. Shelves can be installed to house cards, games and so forth.

If you have two hall closets you are rich! One can be reserved for games and odds and ends, and the other for coats. Even if you have only one a certain amount of space must be reserved for guests' coats. It is a nice idea to keep special coat hangers for guests—pretty ones of red or black velvet that are kept separate from your others.

A Hall in Gloucester

BEFORE we doff our coats and hats in the hall and open the living-room door I would like to describe a few halls that have stuck in my memory. They may give you some notions about your own.

The first one is in a picturesque old house in Gloucester, a town still full of the romance of sailing ships. The floor of the hall is of red brick that is kept softly polished. The walls are white plaster stretching up to a darkly stained, beamed ceiling. At one end of the hall stands an old Dutch cabinet, filled with delightful flowered china. There are two oak side chairs with rush seats, and a rough, woven rush rug is in the center of the brick floor.

DRAMATIC FRONT HALL
Remodeled Inexpensively with Paint and Linoleum

THE PROBLEM   A large old-fashioned front hall with pretentious decorations and ugly beamed ceiling. The problem was to make it a smart and up-to-date hall with a very small expenditure of money.

THE SOLUTION   1. Black-and-white linoleum was laid in a well-scaled, simple design on top of the old-fashioned terrazzo floor.

2. To reduce the height of the ceiling, a dark band was painted below the cornice and the dado was also painted black and white for the same reason. The chimney breast was painted yellow and the rest of the walls gray.

3. The old-fashioned mantelpiece was removed and a bolection molding was put around the opening.

4. The chairs were covered with shiny dark green leather with brass nails.

5. Two heavy square mahogany tables held two handsome large lamps made out of brass umbrella stands with shades made of imported tortoise-shell paper.

6. The big electric clock is fine in scale and is made of white plaster with a carved black wooden eagle over it. By putting all the emphasis on the clock it was unnecessary to have any more decorations.

The leaded, lattice windows have very deep reveals, and the sills are loaded with potted plants. Big prints of clipper ships hang on the white walls.

Although fairly sparsely furnished this hall is as inviting as can be. And it sets the tone for the whole house.

A Modern Georgian Hall

THE FLOOR OF THIS HALL is of black ebony, inlaid with steel in a big herringbone design. The walls are white, with white plasterwork done in relief around the doors and windows. There is a big Chippendale table, and four fine Chippendale side chairs with black leather seats along the walls.

Two black columns hold eighteenth-century white marble busts. A modern reproduction of a Chinese Chippendale mirror hangs over the table, with the frame painted white instead of gold. In it is reflected a big portrait that hangs on the opposite wall—a picture of a dashing eighteenth-century general in a bright red uniform.

This hall is definitely ultra-sophisticated, and since most of the things in it are authentic it is also very expensive. But never be discouraged by this if it appeals to you—you can accomplish almost the same effect with reproductions and the proper color scheme.

A Hall in a Remodeled New England Farmhouse

THIS was a very simple, inexpensive hall. But it was so charming that I remember several things about it even though it is years since I have seen it. The walls were covered with wallpaper that was a delightful all-over pattern of big bunches of cherries. The floor was painted a dark green, and spattered in red and white. There was a very simple, big table, and the two side chairs had both backs and seats completely upholstered in bright green leather.

A French Provincial Hall

THIS HALL was also wallpapered—this time in a toile de Jouy paper. (Since most halls are not overcrowded with furniture I think wallpaper often has a brightening effect.) On the walls were hung several charming old Brittany prints.

The floor was of red tile, and the side chairs were simple. But the main thing you noticed as you stepped in was a beautiful old French Provincial commode, with big brass handles.

A Smart City Hall

As A matter of fact this hall could go anywhere at all, even though I saw it in a city apartment. The floor was covered with a gray carpet and the walls were hung with striped wallpaper, with the stripes at least five inches wide. They were of dark maroon, red and white.

The furniture was all white—I believe it was old furniture that had been given a coat of white paint. But the seats of the side chairs had been upholstered in turquoise and furnished a striking contrast to the red-and-white walls.

Living Rooms

YOU'VE OPENED the front door, crossed the hall and entered what is undoubtedly the most important room in the whole house. It is the family meeting place. It is your stage for entertaining. It is also your own best expression of what you can do with decoration.

Because the living room is so important it has received almost more than its due all through the first half of this book. I have used it as an example in the discussions of color, balance, walls, floors, furniture and lamps. There was so much to say that I can't hope to rehearse all the details here.

The main thing to remember is to be perfectly free in any and every choice you make. There's no such thing as a "correct" living room any more. Today's living room can be anything you want it to be. It can be a combination living room and library. It can be a living room and dining room together. You can turn one corner of a big living room into your sewing room, or your writing room.

People no longer feel that they must have a "drawing room" and a sitting room, too, in order to be elegant. Even the most elaborate Long Island houses today usually have just one big living room, one dining room and sometimes a library. I think this is because we have all discovered that, just as we can only wear one pair of shoes at a time, we can only live in one living room.

Sometimes, of course, it is wonderfully convenient to have a small upstairs living room. But I think this is usually true of very large families who like to have plenty of space into which the children can spill over.

Most of us, if we have two living rooms, will find one of them being neglected just as the stiff, old-fashioned front parlors were. A successful living room should always look as if it got plenty of use. For this reason keep some of your books in the living room even if you have a separate library. And never hesitate to use things that are dear to you because of their associations. Mrs Theodore Roosevelt, who so kindly wrote the introduction to this book, has one of the most interesting homes I know just because she has cleverly made use of the many Roosevelt mementos. As you enter the hall you see, displayed on the walls, the banners of all the different regiments to which Colonel Roosevelt has belonged. And all through the house are unusual souvenirs of the time the Roosevelts spent in the Philippines and in Haiti.

The Roosevelt home is really so fascinating that I feel it will interest you to read an excerpt from a letter written by Alexander Woollcott to Mrs Roosevelt after a visit there:

6—30—38.

. . . . "However, what is on my mind to write you about is that lovely house of yours. My thoughts have revisited it so often that I think of many of its rooms as rooms I already know well.

"At first—in telling someone about it—I tried summing it up as the final and most satisfactory answer to the whole tribe of decorators. To be any good a house must be as self-sprung as a beard. Yours, I said, was as undisputably yours as your toothbrush.

"But that really doesn't tell the story. It is so clearly a part of this house's quality and secret that all the family had hands in the making of it. For instance, so much of its color and character derives from what Ted has done and is. Then Cornelius by lighting up the innards of goddesses, and Grace being at such pains to marry an architect. But you must know a hundred instances for one that I know.

"An analogy haunts me. All the Du Maurier manuscripts are in the Morgan Library. Affixed to one of them—*Trilby*—is an attestation that it is all in his own handwriting except for one passage, to the transcription of which his wife and all his children lent their hands, this as a ceremony of propitiation to their household gods.

"Well, there you are. I haven't really said my say because if I really set down all the elements which in my guess had blessed this work of your hands, I would have to use such words as 'love' and 'goodness' and our generation has lost the trick of using such words.

"I declare that, from sheer force of habit, I've let this letter turn into a review of your work for all the world as though you'd written a new play. Yet why not? It's as authentic an art, and your example of it is certainly a cut above any new play I've seen in recent years except 'Our Town' perhaps.

"Yes, except 'OUR TOWN.' "

*   *   *

Naturally, the Roosevelts have lived a more exciting life than most of us and so their mementos are unique. But don't hesitate to display your own even if they aren't terribly unusual. They are the color of your life and deserve their place.

Then remember your five cardinal virtues—Courage, Color, Balance, Smart Accessories and Comfort—and plan just the living room you want.

There is just one word of warning that I think applies specifically to living rooms—many women are inclined to make them too feminine. Even if you're not married you won't want a living room for ladies only. So here are a few tips on what I've discovered men like in decoration.

Better Quarters for Your Better Halves

MOST MEN like warm color. There are exceptions, of course, but the average man will tell you that the lucid, pale blue dress you love so much looks "washed out" to him, and why don't you wear the red one this evening? Give him a contrasting, rather than a pastel, living room.

Men love to be comfortable. Be sure you have really soft, luxurious upholstered furniture.

Men, as a rule, don't like anything that looks too fragile. Avoid chairs with legs that look as though they would snap off easily, tables or lamps that look tippy and ash trays that are so small you have to be an expert marksman to flick an ash inside.

Many rooms decorated by women are too fussy to make a man feel comfortable. A table that started out to be useful ends up as a stance for china animals. A mantelpiece becomes so crowded with ornaments that there is no room left for a man to lean his elbow on it and exercise his primitive right to warm his back at his own fire. Windows are shrouded by too much fluff. The entire room is so crowded with big and little objects that it's hard to move around or pace the floor.

Most men are miserable if they aren't allowed to litter the living room a bit with their own possessions and toys. They hate having to tuck everything into some inconvenient hideaway the very minute they are through with it.

It's all very well to feed the brute, but if you want him to stick around after dinner think of him when you plan your living room!

A Country Living Room

ALL THIS TALK about men reminds me of one living room I have visited that was designed entirely by a man—an architect. I will describe it, and several others, just to put you in a living-room frame of mind.

I remember it best as I saw it one winter evening when I had arrived from town to spend the week end with my architect friend and his wife.

A huge fire was burning in the grate. The mantelpiece is an exceptionally fine black marble one with two columns. The detail of the room is most distinguished—rather heavy trim of the period of 1830. But no sense of austerity is conveyed by the rest of the room.

It is fairly large—probably twenty-five feet square—with three big windows leading out onto a terrace. Above the long yellow curtains are old-fashioned, carved, gold cornice boards. The walls of the rooms are hung with white paper with gold medallions.

The heavy curtains were drawn back, even though twilight had fallen, so that you could see the snow on the terrace outside and the white marble steps leading up to the wide grass path that passed through the tiny orchard to the octagonal pigeon house.

In the middle of the room was a big round table loaded with books, magazines, several pipes, a bag of knitting and a great bowl of red apples and nuts. The air was sweet with the scent of apples and of flowers. In front of the windows were big pots of pink camellia trees and one white tea olive in full bloom.

There was an old Axminster carpet on the floor, patterned with big bunches of red roses, some old rosewood furniture upholstered in chintz and a couple of big, comfortable, nondescript chairs.

The room was not particularly orderly—it was filled with the litter of pleasant living. Many of the things in it were definitely shabby, for my friends were far from well off at the time. They had a black marble fireplace because they had enough energy to visit a big wrecking company and buy one that had once been in a demolished building. The carved, gold cornice boards they had found at a Baltimore auction when a house and all its fittings went on the block. It costs nothing but patient care to have potted plants that will be healthy all year round. Everything in the room was a tribute to the good taste, rather than the pocketbook, of my hosts. And for this very reason it is a room of infinite charm and distinction.

A Sophisticated Living Room

I KNOW another living room that was essentially designed for entertaining. Whenever the lady who owns it is alone with her husband they prefer to sit upstairs in the library. So she has created a living room that is very dramatic—a stage for parties.

The room is large and very high. The walls are painted dead white. The straight hung curtains are of black-and-white brocade, in a very bold design, and extend from ceiling to floor. The floor is stained black, and is partially covered by a closely clipped fur rug of creamy white.

Opposite the fireplace stands a large sofa, covered in rough white material. Over it hangs a large, rather ornate, Venetian glass mirror. On either side of the sofa is a comfortable upholstered chair in the same black-and-white brocade as the curtains. And right in front of the fire is a round, upholstered hassock, at least four feet in diameter, covered in black-and-white civet cat fur.

The wood furniture is all lacquer—small tables, exquisite little chairs. There is a red lacquer grandfather's clock in one corner of the room that shows up vividly against the black floor and white walls.

One night when I dined there the color scheme was accentuated by quantities of red and white flowers. There were bright geranium blossoms, tightly arranged in flat white Chinese bowls, and high, clear glass vases of white Easter lilies.

This is, of course, a highly stylized, sophisticated room and is certainly not suited to everyone. It does happen to suit its owner to perfection. She has a mass of red hair, which she wears in a bang, a glowing white skin and bright red lips. She loves to wear red, pink or chinese yellow— and fits into her room like a dream.

A Family Living Room

THE WALLS of this pleasant living room are grained to imitate pine. (I happen to know the old painter who did them—he always works in striped trousers and a morning coat!) On the floor is an emerald-green carpet edged with white fringe.

At the windows hang cheerful chintz curtains—bright flowers with many green leaves on a white background. The fireplace is equipped with a hob grate, in which cannel coal is burned—and it is lighted at the drop of a hat. On each side of the fireplace are niches in the wall, filled with lovely old china.

A comfortable sofa and two chairs are upholstered in the same chintz as the curtains, and there are several other easy chairs covered in worn red leather. There is also one big, natural wood, wicker rocker with the seat and back upholstered in green felt.

On one wall stands a funny old grandfather's clock from Maine with a plaid front with a dog painted on it. And in one corner of the room stands baby's discarded high chair, with a flowering plant in the seat instead of Her Majesty who has grown much too big.

The pictures on the walls are all in old-gold and black frames, with wide white mats. An old oak writing table stands between the long windows.

This simple but successful room makes loving use of family possessions. And there always seems to be sunshine in it even when there isn't a ray of it anywhere else.

A Hospitable Living Room

THIS PARTICULAR ROOM is owned by a young career woman who is not yet married. She is a most friendly, attractive girl and loves to return invitations by entertaining informally in her own apartment, usually at tea or cocktail hour.

The walls of her living room are white, but a hunting-pink carpet (hunting pink is actually light lacquer-red) warms them up. The curtains are crisp red taffeta, lined with sprigged chintz. Before the fire is a very low, wide, comfortable sofa upholstered in the same chintz. And in front of that sofa is a low, substantial mahogany table. This table really symbolizes the whole room—it is so generous. It is at least five feet long and three feet wide. It carries two big, serviceable ashtrays and a cigarette box that is always filled with several varieties of cigarettes. There is usually a clear glass vase of flowers at one end and an assortment of new magazines at the other. There is plenty of room to put down a teacup or a highball glass anywhere you please.

Over one end of the sofa is folded a soft cashmere rug, and all sorts of big and little cushions invite you to tuck one behind your back and re-lax. On each side of the fireplace are big, soft chairs, slip-covered to match the sofa. They each have their own footstool and solid, squarish tables beside them.

There are always pots of flowers in the room—in the summer, blue hydrangeas between the red taffeta curtains or blue cornflowers on the big table before the fireplace.

A well-equipped writing table stands behind the sofa, and a perma-nent bridge table is set up and ready to use at another end of the room.

The tea table is always laid, and the sprigged china tea set is charming. There is something very inviting about the glittering china even though guests may have no interest in tea at all, and prefer to go to the sideboard and pour out a good stiff drink.

A Modern Living Room

THIS is a living room owned by a very young, very bright couple. The walls of their room are of light cork, the floor is a very dark brown. Since they spent a good bit of money on the walls they bought the simplest modern furniture they could find—and they bought it unfinished. Then they gave all the wood several coatings of wax and rubbed it until it became a lovely, soft, honey color. The upholstered furniture is all covered in rough beige slip covers. To contrast this honey-and-white furniture there is one note of beautiful color—a huge coffee table covered with flame-colored leather. This table is really the only note of brilliant color in the whole room.

But there are numerous bookshelves worked into the furniture and walls, and the multicolored book bindings provide a real color note. Flowers look heavenly against the cork walls.

There are two especially designed modern cabinets—one to house a radio-phonograph, and one to hold record albums. And the pictures on the walls also express the real interests of the owners of the room. They are all black-and-white prints or lithographs, matted but unframed. The mats can be attached to the walls with special stickers (the sort that are used in window displays) and then the pictures can be changed whenever the spirit moves.

There is a rough off-white rug on the floor. (This isn't as impractical as it sounds—the rug doesn't show the dirt as much as you would expect because the material is so shaggy.)

This very modern room would be cold and office-like in final effect if the lady of the house weren't clever. She realizes that such a severe room needs as many humanizing touches as possible. So she doesn't object to a certain amount of homelike litter in her room. There happens to be a small balcony outside the windows, and she has a row of potted trees growing there so that they can be seen through the windows at all times. The result is as cheerful and lively as you please.

The One-Room Apartment

THE CITY DWELLER who lives in the increasingly popular one-room apartment faces a lot of little problems that arise directly from her lack of space. But she definitely belongs in this chapter because the whole ambition of the one-room apartment is to be *all* living room.

Sofas that turn into regular beds at night and chests of drawers that can serve as roomy bureaus but don't look bedroomy, are obviously musts. If the apartment has a very large closet that can be used as a dressing room everything is much easier. A chest of drawers can often be built right into such a closet, with room left on each side for clothes poles.

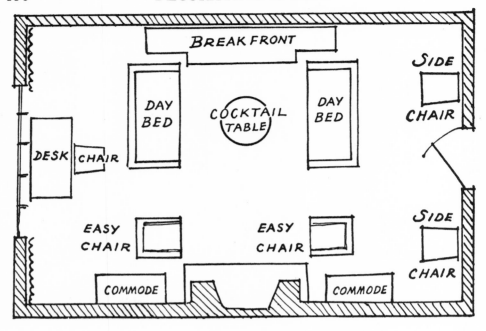

Vigilant neatness must be the watchword in any one-room apartment or the result will be an impression of untidy confusion. Everything has to be put away all the time—so the more closets, poke holes and glory holes you can devise the happier you will be. The drum table, sketched on page 99 in Chapter 8, is a godsend in a small apartment. You can tuck all sorts of things out of sight in a pair of these tables—even pillows, bedding and extra comforters.

A carefully planned layout is also essential. No matter how large your room is you are going to have to put a staggering amount of furniture in it to be comfortable, so it must be very cleverly arranged. The layout above may not fit your particular case exactly, but I am including it in the hope that it may give you a few suggestions.

10

DINING ROOM AND KITCHEN

Eat and Be Merry

No OTHER ROOM in the house has changed so radically during the last twenty-five years as the dining room. Dinner is no longer a rather dull, sacred rite when everyone overeats in an overcrowded room. Modern dining rooms have a much more lighthearted quality to fit more lighthearted, modern dinners.

The first thing that happened to the old-fashioned dining room was to sweep it clear for action. The bulky china cabinet has followed the still earlier plate rail into oblivion. The cumbersome family sideboard, stuffed with odd and unused silver, is also gone. The monster chandelier that hung over the table like the sword of Damocles has disappeared in favor of candles.

Even the tablecloths that used to shroud the most beautiful tables at every meal have been put firmly in their place. You can use them when you want to, and not if you don't. They may appear at breakfast and at very formal dinners. But at lunch and everyday dinners they have given way to place mats.

DINNER FOR EIGHT
Without a Dining Room

THE PROBLEM To entertain eight or ten people comfortably and with chic in a one-room kitchenette apartment which is too small for a dining table.

THE SOLUTION 1. This is the same room which appears in the photograph opposite page 32 and in the frontispiece. The upholstered furniture in the room is all covered in a chintz—a flowered pattern on a white ground at forty-five cents a yard.

2. The big wing chair is deeply tufted in blue Rajah silk, and both front and *back* are tufted in the same way.

3. The curtains are made of the same inexpensive, light Rajah silk of exactly the same sky blue as the walls and wood furniture.

4. Silver candelabra with plain white candles add a dignified note and are enchantingly reflected in the mirrors at night.

5. After the guests have settled themselves comfortably around the living room, the small tables pictured are brought in and placed before them. Each little table is correctly set and can be served just as easily and precisely as if the guests were gathered around one big table. (But the party that results will probably be much gayer and amusing—just because it is informal and different.)

In many houses the dining room has disappeared altogether, and a drop-leaf table in the living room is substituted. If you have abandoned a real dining room and want to have more people for dinner than your living-room table can accommodate here is a suggestion. Get several nests of small tables that can be brought out after your guests have settled down comfortably in various chairs and sofas around the room. Place one little table before each guest. Then they can either be set individually, or trays that are exactly the same size as the tables and have been all set up can be brought out from the kitchen. After this, guests can either help themselves from a buffet table or be served at their own little tables just as correctly as if they were all gathered around one large table. This sort of informal dinner party is often more fun than one given in a big impressive dining room.

You can be formal or informal in today's dining room. But even in a formal dining room you won't want to be ponderous or gloomy. The dining table and its chairs, a serving table, sometimes a sideboard, may be your only furniture. But your color scheme must be planned to make it the merry place it should be. Eating is really one of your indoor sports. You play three times a day, and it's well worth while to make the game as pleasant as possible.

An informal dining room can turn into almost a second living room—with a comfortable sofa and chairs, a writing desk, a tea table before the fireplace, a row of potted plants on the window sills.

My own feeling is that any dining room, whether formal or informal, should have as much sunny out-of-doors quality as possible. This is surely a fine place to put your low stands of bulbs, potted flowering shrubs, your aquarium or your bird cage.

Dining-Room Furniture

As I SAID BEFORE, you probably won't need much more than a table, chairs, serving table and possibly a sideboard, to have a perfectly correct dining room. If you are buying new furniture I advise you not to buy a set of matching pieces. In a room as sparsely furnished as the average dining room this is likely to be dull. Individuality will brighten the room. Even the chairs and table need not match exactly. They should, of course, match in proportion and in general character.

Above everything else try to get really comfortable dining-room chairs. This means that they must be a convenient height for eating, and the seats must have some sort of padding or upholstery. You can't ask anyone to sit through a meal on hard wood and expect them to enjoy it. I have even seen dining chairs recently that were completely upholstered armchairs. They were gloriously comfortable but I'll admit that they did take up a lot of room and limited the seating capacity of the table.

If you are buying a new dining table you will naturally want to get the best-looking one you can afford. But if you are on a limited budget you certainly don't have to spend a fortune on your table. There are so many other places in the house where your money will show more. You will want the table to be steady, of course. There is nothing less conducive to a hearty, pleasant time at dinner than a wiggly table that has to be treated gingerly. And you will want a table that is roomy for you when you are alone and can be extended (with leaves) when you are entertaining. I think round tables are the most practical. They seat more people than square tables of the same size, and if you have a maid service is much easier. One maid can serve eight people seated at a round table without awkwardness, when she couldn't manage it without being very slow if she had to trot around corners. A round dining table that is 55 inches in diameter will seat eight people comfortably. And a good, average height for any dining table is 28½ inches from the floor.

But if you don't feel like investing in a new table there are so many things you can do to your old one. Don't ever be afraid to experiment with old things—some of the smartest effects were achieved because someone used brains instead of money!

You can always put a new top on an old table. Black Carrara glass and mirror are both excellent. Or the new top could be of wood—possibly marbleized. It is still more economical to remove all the old paint or stain, bleach the wood, and then paint it anew. Here are a few painting suggestions for dining tables and chairs:

1. Shiny black with dull gold trim.
2. Dark, seal brown, picked out in gold.
3. Glossy white.
4. Chinese red.
5. Apple green.
6. An exact match for your walls.

It isn't necessary to paint the chairs to match the table unless you want to. You can use mahogany chairs if you have them, or a wood stain on old chairs.

Dining-Room Lighting

Most American dining rooms of thirty or forty years ago were distressingly badly lighted. The center chandelier that was poised perilously over the food threw its harsh light smack into the faces of the diners. Any overhead light of this type is woefully unflattering. It will lengthen your nose, draw black lines from nose to mouth and make your eyes look like burned holes in a blanket. It is worth while fussing with your dining-room lighting until it is both convenient and becoming. After all, you want to serve good talk and a good time at your table as well as good food.

If women could have their own way about it most dining rooms would be lighted solely by the soft glow of candles. There could be four on the table, two candelabras on the sideboard and more around the room in candle wall brackets. But usually there is a man in the case who claims (unfairly) that he is going to choke on a fishbone and hates digging for his food through the pitch dark.

You can, of course, try diminishing the light little by little in the hope that he will not notice it. But usually it is wise to humor him—give him his own way but dish it up your way. You can supplement your candle-light by wiring a bulb into a big bowl in the middle of the sideboard. And two simple standing lamps, placed in opposite corners of the room or at each side of the fireplace, will throw the light up to the ceiling and then scatter it around the room much more pleasantly than the old overhead glare.

Then, too, the dining room is one of the few places in the house where I recommend the use of wall brackets. But don't use just any wall brackets—make them count decoratively. If you shop for brackets that are twice as large as is usual, and twice as good-looking, you will have an asset instead of a liability. If you already have the ordinary, too-small wall brackets paint them the same color as the walls and use inconspicuous, plain paper shades.

China, Silver, Glass and Linen

IN THE SELECTION OF CHINA there are two different schools of thought. Many people like to vary the china from course to course. Others hold out for complete sets. I happen to favor sets, but that doesn't mean that I'm right.

The important thing to remember is that everything on your table is just as much of an "accessory" and just as important as the accessories in your living room. Plan them carefully, combining their decorative effect and the jobs they have to do.

China, for instance, is made to serve food on. So many people forget this and buy something that is beautiful in itself but doesn't act as a grateful frame for the food it carries. When you select your plates try to visualize crisp salads, green vegetables and roast beef!

There is an enormous variety of good china on the market today. Faithful copies of the old English designs (which in some strange way seem to fit in with both old and modern settings), and copies of Spode, Coalport, Crown Derby, Staffordshire, Lowestoft and Wedgwood are all easily obtainable. So are beautiful designs in Dresden and other European china. The modern designers definitely deserve your attention—they are turning out lovely patterns in France, Denmark, Sweden, and right here at home in America. Whatever you select, it is always wise to buy an open stock so that replacements can be made easily.

Silver

ASIDE from your flat silver there is much less silver in the modern dining room than ever before. You can, of course, get a most luxurious effect if your candlesticks, candelabra, salt and pepper shakers, tea set and small nut or candy dishes are of silver. (Modern copies of old Sheffield are unusually lovely.) But you don't have to use silver at all—you can have everything of china or glass if you want to and save all that endless polishing. A whole set of Corning glass is tremendously effective.

If you are buying new flat silver you will be offered a bewildering array of beautiful designs. Copies of the early Georgian or American Colonial patterns are excellent. So is the more simple, modern silver that is being made in Denmark, Sweden and America.

When you buy new silver don't be harassed by a salesman into buying all sorts of different forks, special bouillon spoons, orange spoons and so forth. They are entirely a matter of choice. You can use an ordinary teaspoon for soup in a cup, a teaspoon for oranges and a large spoon shaped like your serving spoons for soup in a plate.

If you can't find a pattern you like in your local stores, you can always write directly to the big silver companies who advertise in the magazines and ask for a catalogue. And when you have selected a pattern, buy open stock just as you did in china.

If you have old silver and have been made unhappy about it because it is old-fashioned, just forget the criticism. There isn't the slightest necessity for silver to match the décor of the dining room in period. Neither need you worry if your flat silver is in a totally different design from your tea or coffee set. As long as the silver is beautiful in line and ornament any other considerations are of relative unimportance.

Glass

NOTHING IS LOVELIER than beautiful old glass. But in this day of hustle, bustle and breakage I do think it is rash to spend much money on authenticity in anything so fragile. The copies of Waterford, Georgian and old English glass will be almost as effective and so much more practical. And so much modern glass is exceptionally fine.

If you are buying new glass, crystal is usually a wiser choice than colored glass unless you definitely need a note of color in your room. Crystal will give you more freedom in your use of color elsewhere on your table, and most liquids look prettier in crystal than in anything else.

Linens

LINENS are something in which the average woman takes great pride and needs very little advice. But even linens have felt the modern urge toward informality. White damask cloths, which used to be the only thing, are often used only for the most formal occasions. Especially if your table top is beautiful will you want to take advantage of the vogue for place mats or doilies.

You can have a lot of fun being original about your place mats. They can be made of practically anything, and they are the simplest sort of job to do yourself. They can be made of any shade of colored linen, heavy cotton, lace, in solid colors with white borders, in checks or in plaids. I saw one new set of place mats the other day that were made of crisp organdy in an allover sprig design. Usually, however, the simpler they are, the better. Excellent ones can be made of solid colored linen with your own initials in one corner. (Have the initials very large, though—at least 2½ inches high.)

For out-of-doors dining and informal meals, the so-called peasant linens are perfect. They come in every conceivable color and design. Just be careful not to be carried away in the stores by one that is so very bright and multicolored that it would need an all-white room to carry it without clashing. Solid colored ones with wide, white hems will give you more latitude in the rest of your color scheme.

Decorating the Table

HERE'S where you can indulge all your love of variety and experiment. After you have laid the table, the center of it is an open challenge at every meal.

When you are in a hurry, an old English, covered silver dish, or a Lowestoft bowl, will dress it up in two seconds. When you have more time there are any number of amusing centerpieces you can create.

1. A flat bowl, with blossoms floating on the surface of the water. (Flowers from a tall bouquet can often be revived by dissolving half an aspirin tablet in the water and used in this way when they are too far gone to stay in a vase.)

2. Six tiny, china vases, set in a circle and filled with tight little bouquets.

3. Six small, clear glass bottle vases arranged in a circle and holding one rose apiece.

4. A low china bowl of ivy.

5. A bowl of fruit of contrasting colors—apples, tangerines and a pineapple.

6. A wooden bowl of well-scrubbed vegetables arranged in a great bouquet.

When you have a party you can be a bit unusual if you want to. (It will give your guests something to help the table talk over the first hurdles.) I went to one dinner party where the hostess had decorated the center of her long table with a large apothecary's scale of shiny brass— the sort of scale in which brass pans hang by chains from a black-and-brass center column. She had placed a low dish on each pan with an equal amount of water and nasturtium blossoms, so that the pans balanced exactly.

There is really only one warning about table decorations—keep them low enough so that you don't hide people on the other side of the table. Otherwise, cut loose and enjoy yourselves!

Color Scheme and Decoration of the Dining Room

THE COLOR SCHEME for your dining room should be worked out in just the same way as that of your living room. There is no special rule that says certain colors are appropriate for dining rooms and others are not. But because your dining room is usually not overcrowded with furniture, and also because you don't live in it as much as you do in other rooms, you can often be more dramatic there than elsewhere. I will describe a few dining rooms that may give you suggestions for your own.

A Simple, Cheerful Dining Room

THIS IS A ROOM that anyone could have—anywhere. The furniture is all painted white, and the seats of the chairs are upholstered in blue. (The glossy white table makes food look particularly tempting.) The walls are papered with wallpaper that has a delft-blue-and-white pattern, and white muslin curtains hang at the windows.

The carpet is a bright cherry red. And on the window sill of the biggest window stands a row of potted primroses.

An Informal Dining Room in the Country

ONE of the most enchanting, informal dining rooms I know belongs to a very fortunate friend of mine who has a fine country estate. The dining room is actually an addition to the house—the connecting link between the old Colonial house and a later wing. It has windows on both sides and a low ceiling. The entire room is sheathed in pine boards, and the few pictures are old family portraits.

An intimate group surrounds the fireplace—a couple of worn red leather chairs and an overstuffed sofa covered in a highly glazed chintz with a flower pattern.

The dining-room furniture proper is mahogany, which shows up beautifully against pine walls.

One end of the room opens onto a sun porch, enclosed, and furnished with Early American pieces. The other end, facing south, opens right into the greenhouse, and the perfume of the flowers drifts into the dining room both summer and winter.

A Small City Dining Room

YOU DON'T NEED a country estate and a greenhouse to create an unusual dining room, however. I know one dining room owned by a young New York woman of modest income which is just about perfect.

The room itself is very small and would seem like a box with a big table in it unless handled cleverly. But my friend has ingeniously turned her square little room into a round one by hanging the walls with an inexpensive, sea-green material, gathered very full and suspended from a great wooden hoop nailed right under the ceiling and cutting off all the corners. To carry the idea still further the dining table is round, too. The legs are painted the color of the walls, and it has a mirror top.

In the window of the room stands a large aquarium full of goldfish and little coral trees. This is lighted at night by electric-light bulbs concealed behind and below it. The whole effect of the room is that of some lovely underwater world.

The last time I dined there the mirror table top was concealed by a deep cream cloth of that new material that looks like expensive satin damask but is actually made of rayon and linen. Big napkins matched the cloth, with large monograms in deeper cream. Four candlesticks held tall white candles on the table, and the centerpiece wa a low crystal bowl of water lilies. The flat silver was modern and the china was luster with a design in silver and gray.

The whole room is comparatively inexpensive, but because real imagination went into it the final effect is one of remarkable distinction and good taste.

A Conservative Dining Room

As AN EXAMPLE of a more formal dining room I'm immodest enough to say that I can't think of anything better than a room I arranged for a friend of mine who lives in New York and entertains a great deal.

The room has white walls and ceiling, and the floor is stained such a dark brown that it is practically black. There is a black mantelpiece with big brass andirons and fender. Red brocade is used for the curtains, which hang in voluminous folds to the floor. The seats of the dining chairs are upholstered in the same material.

The room is lighted by very large, carved, gilded wood wall brackets, topped by a black eagle with wings outspread. They are copies of an old eighteenth-century design that follows the Georgian tradition and are very effective with the early eighteenth-century English mahogany furniture in this particular room.

The room has two niches in the walls, one on each side of the mantelpiece. The shelves are cut in a scalloped design and edged with gilt paint. The niches are painted a very dark green and filled with china.

This type of dining room is in the best American tradition. It always has great dignity and charm. The small dining room at the White House, as a matter of fact, is another example of the same type and period.

Your Own Dining Room

PLEASE don't be dismayed if several of these dining rooms sound so expensive and so elaborate that you know you can't possibly duplicate them. You might not want to even if you could. And you can do almost everything you do want to do with a little money and a lot of imagination.

If you haven't a fireplace in your dining room you may have a near-by flue that can be tapped for a small Franklin stove. Or you can defy your lack of chimney altogether and buy one of the imitation fireplaces discussed in Chapter 4. They may not throw out real heat—but they do throw out very real cheer.

If you haven't any authentic black lacquer furniture, and have your heart set on a color scheme that includes a red carpet, flowered wallpaper, green moiré curtains and black lacquer furniture, remember that can of black paint I'm always talking about.

You may have some lovely china that just sits uselessly in some closet. You can display it at very small expense on a pair of hanging shelves.

If you can't afford much furniture at all, turn your attention to your color scheme. You can actually "furnish" your dining room with beautiful color.

Kitchens

A FEW YEARS AGO the efficiency experts finally got into the kitchens. There they all crawled around on their hands and knees with tape measures in the throes of the step-saving fad. When they got all through they usually announced that you could save four and one half inches of walking distance by switching all the major units around at the mere cost of three hundred dollars.

Of course all of their recommendations weren't silly. And the result is that most modern kitchens are models of sparkling efficiency. This is certainly all to the good. But I think the concentration on efficiency has often meant the sacrifice of other things. So many kitchens today look like hospital corridors—white and cold.

The kitchen should really be one of the jolliest rooms in the house as well as the most efficient. When it is cheerful and attractive it is almost irresistible. If you have ever tried the experiment of throwing your kitchen doors open to your guests I am sure you have found this to be true. It's impossible to shoo them back into the living room again! A midnight icebox-raiding party after the theater is ten times more fun than the same thing in a formal restaurant.

If you do your own work you certainly deserve the nicest kitchen you can think of. And you can really let yourself go when you plan its color scheme. In a dark kitchen it is true that you will help your lighting problem by sticking to white walls and a white ceiling. But unless the room is really dark you certainly don't have to. There is so little ornamentation in a kitchen that you can get wonderful results with almost primitive color combinations.

1. You might try lemon-yellow walls, white woodwork, and white linoleum, edged with a border of red, on the floor. Then you could paint the insides of the closets with green and edge the shelves with red.

2. Pale blue walls with white woodwork look lovely and cool in a kitchen. With them you could have a black linoleum floor and the closet interiors in bright red. Red-and-white-checked gingham curtains, red-bordered dish towels and pots of red geraniums on the window sills would finish the picture.

3. One of the cheeriest kitchens I know was designed by the Norwegian cook whose mistress very sensibly consulted her on the subject since she is queen of the kitchen most of the time. She chose

white walls, blue woodwork, a lacquer red-painted floor and two whacking big travel posters of fjords which she got free from a Scandinavian steamship line.

4. Another country kitchen I know is so homelike that it really implores you to sit down and have a cup of tea right there. It has walls of wide pine boards, a red brick floor, curtains of rough yellow linen, a gate-legged oak table and four chairs with rush seats. The linen tablecloths used are of the same yellow as the curtains.

My own inclination is always toward a comfortable, country sort of kitchen. If you have room for it by all means have an upholstered chair or rocker by the window. Also a table and chairs where you can have breakfast or a midnight snack occasionally. So often there is nothing inviting to sit down on in a kitchen, and there are frequently small oases in preparing a meal when you can sit down and take a breather, or pick up a bit of knitting, while you keep an eye on the stove. Keep a magazine rack for books and periodicals or a small radio in the kitchen, too. Your kitchen can be the most convenient workshop in the world and still be the sort of place that suggests a jolly fudge-making party or an old-fashioned taffy pull.

11

BEDROOMS AND BATHS

One Third of Your Life!

SOME LIGHTNING CALCULATOR whiled away an idle moment one day by figuring out that the average person spends one third of her life in bed. Even if you don't sleep a full eight hours every night, I'll wager that you do spend that third of your life in your bedroom—either sleeping, reading in bed, resting or dressing.

Certainly, then, your bedroom deserves to be the most comfortable, attractive place you can possibly make it. Many people aren't nearly as comfortable in their bedrooms as they might be. And it's not because they need a great deal of money to spend there—it is just because they haven't given the question any thought at all. You may concentrate on appearances all through the rest of your house, but in the bedrooms comfort should be supreme.

I think that bedrooms should also be very intimate rooms—they should express your personal preferences in every way. Use your favorite colors in your bedroom, hang the picture you love better than any other where you can see it the minute you open your eyes in the morning. Your bedroom is the perfect place for your dearest keepsakes and souvenirs, for cleverly framed snapshots of your family, for trinkets you have picked

153

up somewhere and kept because they remind you of something happy. Of all the rooms in the house your bedroom is *yours*. This is true even if you share it with your husband. All that means is that you must make room in the bedroom for his things as well as your own.

But let's get back to comfort. The place where this is most important is obviously your bed.

Beds and Their Accessories

WHEN you buy a box spring and mattress it is really folly to be too economical. Here you are dealing with something that is closely related to your good health, to say nothing of your good temper. By all means get a well-made inner spring mattress and a good box spring. They are not nearly as expensive as they used to be, and if turned once a week and completely renovated every eight to ten years they will be luxuriously comfortable for practically a lifetime.

The bed frame that you use for your spring and mattress can be whatever you prefer.

1. *Four-Posters:* Personally I love four-poster beds and consider them the most decorative choice of all. They can be made with either a straight or barrel top and draped in any way you please. If you find a picture of a four-poster that you like, your local carpenter can copy it for you perfectly well. It isn't in the least necessary that it be an antique. I must admit, however, that they are slightly more expensive than other bed frames. There is so much more to the wooden frame and then they have to be draped.

2. *Beds with upholstered or padded headboards:* Beds of this type give an effect of great comfort and luxury and can also be made to order according to your own design. They do present a cleaning problem,

though, and if upholstered the upholstery must be renewed occasionally.

3. *Plain wooden beds:* These are the conventional bed frames stocked by every department store. You can buy them in copies of every known period and in every known style. They are the least expensive of all but they are also the least original or decorative.

4. *Modern beds:* These are usually made to order, and the unfinished furniture stores specialize in them. In one way they are great fun, for you can have them made to suit your particular requirements—have a shelf for books built right into the frame, for instance, or a night table with deep drawers built onto the side of the bed.

The page of sketches illustrates various types of beds in detail. A good thing to remember about all beds is that they definitely don't need to be the conventional natural wood—mahogany or walnut or maple. They can be painted any color you please. It is often a good idea to paint a bed a fairly light color—it makes it seem to take up less space. (Notice the white four-posters in the photograph opposite page 166 in this chapter.) Fashions change slightly, of course, but at the moment it is smart to paint bedsteads the same color as the walls.

Most decorators agree that a double bed really looks better in a room than twin beds. If you are the sort of person who must have a bed to yourself there are clever, modern twin beds that are made with one headboard. They look like a double bed in the daytime and swing apart at night. They take up much less room than twin beds, too.

Bed Accessories

THESE are almost as important to the comfort of your bed as are the box spring and mattress. And here is where so many people slip up and don't do everything they could do for themselves.

There are so *many* things you need to be really happy in bed!

1. A good reading lamp—perhaps a gooseneck with a high-powered bulb, perhaps one of those little spotlights that throw the light right on your book.
2. An adequate end table (one at each side of the bed if possible).
3. A small radio on the table.
4. A bedside clock, perhaps with a luminous dial.
5. A thermos for ice water or hot cocoa.
6. A jar of cookies or fruit for night nibblers.
7. An outlet for an electric pad when you want one.
8. A bedside telephone and a complete list of telephone numbers.
9. A small book, or magazine, rack for night reading.
10. An ash tray and cigarette box.
11. Just the pillows you really find most comfortable. (Perhaps one hard and one soft and one baby pillow.)
12. A good supply of blankets of all weights.
13. A comfortable, pretty breakfast tray and china, for breakfast in bed or for use when you're ill.

Think of all the little things that you usually have to hop out of bed for—and then install them within reach if you possibly can. I know one person who has an unusually well-equipped bed, and she explained it to me laughingly:

"Once I had grippe in a particularly barren hotel bedroom," she told me. "After five days of being helplessly uncomfortable, irritated and bored to tears, I decided that I would never let that happen again. Now whenever I arrange a bedroom I ask myself whether it is the best possible place in which to be ill with grippe! I've never had grippe since then, but it's a good system."

BEDROOM DETAILS
Wallpaper, Stripes, Quilted Linen, Leatherette, Carpet

THE PROBLEM To select bedroom fabrics that would harmonize pleasantly and not conflict with a delightful but very busy flowered wallpaper.

THE SOLUTION 1. The wallpaper in this room is an extremely bold, allover pattern of pale and deep pink roses and large dark green leaves on a white background.

2. The carpet chosen is specially dyed gray with a mauve undertone which picks out certain mauvish-gray tints in the buds of the wallpaper flowers.

3. The chair is covered in brilliant green-and-gray striped satin.

4. The bedspreads and dressing table skirt are made of plain gray quilted linen.

5. The glass curtains are of transparent white muslin hung very simply and gathered a full one hundred percent. A big white flower pattern is woven right into the muslin. (This same idea would be charming in an allover pattern of white polka dots—huge ones the size of silver dollars.)

6. No overcurtains are used, but the windows are framed with the same gray quilted material used for bedspreads and dressing table.

7. The beds are of bright green leatherette with large, shiny chromium nails.

8. The quilts are green taffeta lined with an inconspicuous small-patterned chintz.

Bedroom Furniture

THE AMOUNT OF FURNITURE you put into your bedroom depends of course on what sort of bedroom you want. You may want a sort of bed-sitting-room, in which case you will include a desk, several comfortable chairs and a coffee table. You may want a completely intimate bedroom with nothing but bedroom furniture. In this case, the first thing you will decide is whether you want a dressing table or not.

1. *Dressing tables:* Dressing tables seem to me something of a hangover from the old days when milady sat down and brushed her long hair the prescribed hundred strokes a night. She didn't make up in those days so it didn't matter whether the table was well lighted, and it could be as dainty as it pleased.

Nowadays so many women have short hair that brushing is almost a lost art. And almost all women make up. That means that the modern dressing table must be brilliantly lighted, and it must also be able to stand up under the make-up process—which is usually a fairly messy business. Great jars of creams, lotions, face packs, brilliantines and so forth really belong in the bathroom. And even when there is a good dressing table in the bedroom I think that is where they usually end up. The bathroom light is almost always excellent for make-up purposes, and many women prefer to do it there, standing up.

So a dressing table is usually more decorative than useful. Have one, by all means, if you have room for it, for it can contribute a very charming feminine note in any bedroom. But if your bedroom is small I really don't think it a necessity. If you do have a dressing table, be sure it is large enough. (See photograph opposite page 158.) Dressing tables can be draped in any of various styles:

a. Three very full ruffles of organdy or dotted muslin tied up with bows across the top in a bright contrasting ribbon, tacked on an inexpensive wooden frame. The top could be mirrored or could be a sheet of glass over the same material.

b. On the same frame you could use a long skirt of quilted material, cut on the bias like a swing skirt, edged with an inch-wide band of contrasting color.

c. The table could be shaped like a kneehole desk, made entirely of mirror and undraped. (There are many other undraped styles, too.)

2. *Chests of drawers:* These you will need no matter what sort of bedroom you have. The average woman really needs two—one for underclothes, stockings and handbags, and one for sweaters and outdoor clothes that can't be hung up in the closet. If you have a small room, or must supply a husband with his share of drawer space, chests-on-chests are a practical solution.

If possible, buy two chests just alike and place them with an eye to the symmetry of your room. Their color, hardware and general style will depend on the room as a whole.

But here let me make a plea against *sets* of bedroom furniture. Just as in the dining room they are almost always dull. Select individual pieces that look well together—it doesn't matter a bit whether they match in period so long as size and color are right.

3. *Bedroom chairs:* Even in a small bedroom you will need at least two straight chairs and one very comfortable chair, or chaise longue. If you haven't room for a chaise longue supply the comfortable chair with an ottoman and possibly a ratchet back that can be slanted so that you can really stretch out in it. Every bedroom needs some place where you can rest without actually going to bed.

4. *An end table for your comfortable chair:* Your comfortable bed-

room chair or chaise longue needs an end table just as much as the sofa in your living room. And just the same rules apply to that end table—it should be as large as possible and just the height of the arm of the chair. There you can keep a lamp, an ash tray, your knitting, a vase of flowers or any small photographs that you love.

5. *Bedside tables:* These tables, also, should be as large as possible—if you like even half the accessories we listed you'll need plenty of space! And the drawers should be on a level with the top of the mattress for easy reaching.

6. *Desk:* This of course is optional. Personally, I love a sort of combination bedroom-and-upstairs-sitting-room and always keep my private writing desk in my bedroom. If you do have one remember all the hints I gave about its decoration and arrangements in the chapter on Wood Furniture.

7. *Hanging bookshelves:* These, too, are not necessities, but I think a pair of them always look well in bedrooms. And so many people read in bed nowadays that they are a real convenience in a room where there usually isn't room for a real bookcase.

Blankets and Linen

I'M AFRAID I'm a bit conventional about blankets—I prefer them white or pale pink. But that doesn't mean that you can't get lovely effects with colored blankets that fit in with the color scheme in your room.

The most important thing is to have them large, light and warm. You'll be most comfortable if you have two weights in blankets—they make them today in heavy winter weights and in the sheerest gossamer for summertime.

I don't believe in anything elaborate when it comes to sheets and pil-

lowcases either. Linen sheets are much more expensive than percale, and
frankly I prefer the feeling of percale. I do believe in quality, however.
Your linen should last for years and years, and I would much rather spend
money on quality than on embroidery or fancy designs. A good big
monogram—four to five inches at least—is the smartest thing you can put
on your sheets, with simple hemstitching above the hem.

If you buy colored sheets it is even more important to buy good ones.
If you don't they will wash out to faded, nondescript colors in no time.
Usually I think plain white sheets look best of all, and they are certainly
the most practical. I will admit, however, that I saw some maroon sheets
with big white monograms that were very effective. Of course, if you
like to pamper yourself about your bed linen you can buy very beautiful
crepe-de-Chine sheets, either in solid colors or covered with a dainty
sprigged flower design.

Really, there are two ways to handle the sheet question. Either you
buy a fine quality of white linen or percale and then forget the whole
matter for years and years, or you go in for the novelties of the moment
—colored sheets, silk sheets and so forth—and expect to make replacements fairly frequently.

Quilts and Comforters

THE QUILT OR COMFORTER that is folded over the end of your bed is
almost always on display. For this reason it should be planned both for
comfort and for its decorative contribution.

For comfort's sake be sure it is big enough to hang well down over the
sides of the bed. And be sure that it is not too thick and heavy. So many
comforters are heavy and so small that they slip and slide all over the bed.

From the decorative point of view your comforter can strike any note you please. You may want to use it to give a touch of bright color—a puff of green, red or gray taffeta would look lovely lined with sprigged chintz. Or you may want to keep it a chaste white quilted satin on one side and line it with bright red velveteen on the other. White plush makes an excellent comforter cover and isn't too expensive. Or you can be a bit extravagant and have an exquisitely feminine comforter of white maribou lined with white or pink satin.

Bedroom Closets

THE ARRANGEMENT of closet space is something that should bring out the business executive in every woman. A well-organized closet means so much in convenience, the economical care of your clothes and your appearance.

Every closet really has to be tackled as a separate problem, for everything depends on its particular shape and size. But there is one trick I've found that makes the organization of any closet easier. That is to divide your clothes according to the height they will require when hanging. Evening clothes, for instance, are longer than daytime dresses and need a higher pole. Dressing jackets, sports jackets and blouses can be hung on a much lower pole than daytime dresses. So instead of using just one long pole, with all lengths mixed up on it, and wasting the space below your jackets and short clothes, you can keep all short clothes together and have shelves for hats built over them or shelves for shoes built under them.

If you are fortunate and are living in a house with plenty of closet space (the dream of every good housekeeper) you can create a miracle of orderly arrangement, even reserving one closet for summer things in wintertime and for winter things in the summer. This closet can be permanently moth-proofed. And you can set aside one small closet in each bedroom to house the linen and blankets for that particular room. If you are building your own house you can make yourself that fortunate person by planning your closets with care.

It is possible to make any closet very attractive by keeping it neat as a new pin, even if you go no farther. But you can buy ruffled, colored strips to put on the edges of your shelves if you want to. Then your hat stands, coat hangers and shelf edges can all match. Or you can simply have the shelf edges painted some color that contrasts the wall color, or shiny black. The inside of the closet can be painted or papered to match your bedroom if you choose. Or it can contrast the bedroom color brightly and cheer you up every time you open the door.

A closet will immediately look a bit dressed up if you do as simple a thing as having all your hangers match—perhaps all black velvet. And if you like to keep a laundry bag hanging in your bedroom closet for your personal laundry, have a good-looking linen one with a big monogram on it.

A visit to any department store "Closet Shop" will send you away with your head fairly buzzing with all the new gadgets whose sole object in life is to make your closet a miracle of efficiency and good looks. There are all sorts of garment bags, shoe racks and hat stands—even cellophane hatboxes. Straight nickel rods are manufactured today to replace the old-fashioned closet hooks. They are a great improvement for they are six or seven inches long and will carry three or four dresses on hangers. You can put one on the door of your closet for clothes that are ready to go to the tailor, one in the back of the closet for umbrellas and one on the side for fur pieces that shouldn't be jammed in too tightly against other clothes.

Bathrooms

IF YOU HAVE a big, elaborate bathroom and plenty of money to spend on it you can, of course, run riot with mirrors, black Carrara glass, white fur rugs and beautiful dressing tables. But I won't pretend for a moment that this sort of luxurious bath-dressing-room isn't very expensive.

For most of us a slick, workmanlike bathroom is the most desirable thing within reach. Bathroom tiling comes in all sorts of colors but personally I think cool, pale colors or plain white are the best selections. A bathroom tiled in a hot, heavy color just doesn't seem refreshing enough.

If you have plaster walls, except for tiling around the tub, you can get excellent effects by painting them plain white and then stenciling a bold design on them, perhaps a big green bow or big pink nosegay.

It is also possible to paint or paper bathrooms (washable paper) to match your bedroom. The whole wall can be papered or painted, and the section around the tub protected from splash marks by a big sheet of clear glass or mirror.

If you haven't got a glassed-in shower you will find a really delirious assortment of shower curtains in any department store. You can create just as much effect with your shower curtain as you can with your living-room curtains! A sea-green shower curtain of that material that looks like cellophane will make the simplest bathroom look crisp as a lettuce leaf.

If you have a choice in the tiling of your bathroom floor try shiny black as a contrast to the white walls and fixtures. If it isn't tiled you can get the same effect with solid black linoleum or rubber tiling.

On the whole, it's a good idea to keep your bathroom color scheme simple and definite. One good color against the white of the room is usually enough. That color, and its pattern, can be very bold—just don't scramble two or three patterns in what is usually a pretty small room.

TWIN FOUR-POSTERS
How to Lighten Bulky Furniture with Paint

THE PROBLEM   To use twin four-posters in such a way that the final effect is light and uncrowded.

THE SOLUTION   1. The four-posters selected are a simple adaptation of a Chippendale design. (They could be carried out by almost any carpenter.) In order to eliminate the massive, bulky look of so many four-posters they are painted white instead of the conventional mahogany.

2. The beds are hung with a gathered valance of fresh chintz—pink roses with blue ribbons on a white ground. This is lined with white.

3. The bedspreads are pink, and the comforters are of gray taffeta lined with sprigged chintz.

4. The carpet is a soft gray.

5. The curtains are rough white material lined with pink, and trimmed with wide white wool fringe.

6. The walls are hung with powder-blue-and-white striped wallpaper. (The effect could have been improved, I think, if the wallpaper had been omitted over the window. The space between the top of the window and the ceiling might have been painted plain white—then the Venetian blinds could have been hung from the ceiling right to the floor instead of inside the window embrasure, and the curtains could have added height to the room by hanging all the way from ceiling to floor.)

7. The hardware on the furniture and the lamps is chromium.

8. The stool is covered in cherry-red quilted linen.

9. Notice the comfortable ottoman before the armchair. (The back of this chair can be slanted back so that it takes the place of a chaise longue.)

10. The dressing table is very large, and the top is of mirror. The skirt is cut on the bias, with a large flounce. It is trimmed with red taffeta.

Towels, bath mats, shower curtains, cosmetic jars and medicine cabinet accessories should all play integrated parts in the bathroom scheme.

There are almost as many convenient bathroom gadgets on the market today as there are closet gadgets. I think the most useful of all is the detachable closet, called a Servidor, that can be fastened to any bathroom door. Hanging shelves can supplement both medicine cabinet and Servidor and they have the added advantage of allowing you to add another touch to your color scheme.

Bedroom and Bathroom Decoration in General

NATURALLY, all the rules about color and balance and freedom of choice apply to the bedroom just as well as to the living room or dining room. You can have any color combinations you really like in a bedroom. You can hang any curtains you want there and you can do as you please about the floor. But because it is a place for sleep and rest most people prefer to keep it fresh and unfussy in general appearance.

Do go upstairs and take a real look at your bedrooms. Notice whether they are really comfortable. Notice whether you have planned them for pleasant living. They deserve such planning just as much as any other room in the house.

I shall describe a few bedrooms here—more because we are on the subject than because I think you should accept them as unchangeable models. (And because I like to think of bathrooms as actual adjuncts of bedrooms I'll describe them at the same time.) Some of the rooms were expensive —some extremely inexpensive. The money spent is never the important thing. The all-important essential is just the sort of thought you can give your own rooms on your own budget.

An Inexpensive Summer Bedroom

THIS ROOM WAS ARRANGED by a very smart young woman who made up for lack of money by barrels of energy and originality.

The walls of her bedroom are the palest shade of lemon yellow—the color of spring sunshine. She painted her twin four-poster beds exactly the same color. And since she had spent a fair amount of money on those beds she bought unfinished furniture for the rest of the room and painted that pale yellow too.

The barrel-top four-posters set the tone for the whole room—they are hung with yards and yards of sprigged white muslin. It is the most inexpensive sort of muslin, but there is so much of its crisp, billowing freshness that the beds look delightfully fluffy and airy. The windows are hung with simple curtains of the same material.

There is a big chaise longue in the room and one easy chair—both slip-covered in white bath toweling with white cotton fringe welted into all the seams.

There is no carpet on the floor at all except for small, rough white rugs beside each bed. The floor itself has been painted shiny white and the owner of the room herself stenciled a big design on it in gray.

She is mildly artistic (took up painting last year for the first time) so she has made her own pictures. They are water colors of flowers—but the size is dashing. Each flower must be six inches big. She has mounted them in very wide white mats and not framed them at all—just attached them to the walls with clips.

The seats and backs of the straight chairs are upholstered in very bright light green. The lamps are big cider jugs painted white and fitted with big white shades.

Near the chaise longue is a low, round coffee table and on it there is always a big pot of flowers. When I saw it last the pot held three magenta cyclamens.

The wide main window of the room opens right onto a sun deck (the top of the garage). A white Venetian blind can slant the rays of sunshine in the morning—and there seems to be plenty of sunshine in this bedroom even at midnight.

The Bath

THE BATHROOM that adjoins this bedroom goes right on with the color scheme of the bedroom itself.

There is white linoleum on the floor, a gray and black bathroom rug and a simple white shower curtain. The walls are painted the same yellow as the bedroom and all the fixtures are white.

Two hanging, mirrored shelves serve as a dressing table and the jars and bottles on them are the same bright green as the leather chairs in the bedroom.

A Luxurious Bedroom

THIS ONE is really a bedroom to dream about—the perfect setting for a princess in a fairy story.

The walls are hung with most unusual Chinese antique wallpaper. The background is moss green and carries a design of the Tree of Life. The climbing, spreading branches are covered with dark green leaves and creamy white flowers and an occasional bird has a touch of coral on his wings.

The black floor is covered almost entirely with a very thick, rough, white rug.

The mantelpiece is of carved wood and painted creamy white. The top of the mantelpiece is decorated with a row of white Chinese porcelain figures.

The furniture in the room is a blend of English eighteenth-century mahogany and walnut pieces.

But it is the bed which really dominates the room. It is a double four-poster with a richly carved top in Chinese Chippendale design. The posts also are carved and they look like bunches of bamboo shoots bound to-gether. The bed has been painted a soft white and hung with a corded material that has been dyed to match the background green of the wall-paper. The shaped valance around the top of the bed is trimmed with large chunky silk fringe of the same color. And the inside of the bed valance and the curtains, which fall to the floor, are lined with old green brocade.

The bedspread is of the same green brocade and the part that covers the pillows is a lovely piece of eighteenth-century embroidery in soft colors that pick up the green of the wallpaper and the touches of coral in it.

The big chaise longue is covered in the same corded material as the outside of the bed draperies, with heavy fringe outlining the back and arms. A white swansdown rug, lined with white satin, is thrown over its foot, and the little pillows are of the same material as the upholstery.

The curtains are the same corded material as the outside bed draperies and are bound with the same chunky fringe. They are very long and lie on the floor in lush folds. The reveals of the windows are deep, and lined with mirrors so that they reflect the tall trees outside.

The Bath

THIS IS a true bath-dressing-room. The floor is of zenitherm—a substance that is similar to marble but is not cold to the touch. Its design is black and cream.

The walls are papered just like the bedroom and sheets of clear glass protect them around the bathtub.

At one end of the bathroom stands a dressing table that is shaped like a kneehole desk and made entirely of mirror. It has an adjustable three-face mirror and is brilliantly lighted.

There is one small rug on the floor of the same rough, deep, white material as that in the bedroom.

The bathroom is really so lovely, that when the bedroom door stands open and the wallpaper can be seen in both rooms the effect is just that of an extension of the bedroom.

On the whole, both bedroom and bath are so romantic—so beautiful—that I am afraid the harsh outside world would be too much for me if I owned them. I would take to my bed and never get up again!

A Child's Bedroom

THIS BEDROOM belongs to a little girl of ten. Everything in it is as simple as can be but the effect of the room is as charming as its young owner's taffy-colored pigtails.

The walls are hung with paper that has a white background covered with green ivy leaves forming a trellis pattern. Crossed white muslin curtains hang at the windows and all the woodwork is painted white.

At one end of the room is a maple double-decker bed. (Although this young lady has her room to herself she has reached the age where all little girls adore having their friends stay overnight.)

There are two straight maple chairs and two small but comfortable upholstered chairs. The upholstered chairs are slip-covered in patchwork quilting in a bright design of reds and greens. Quilting sounds extravagant for a child's room but this particular job is a tribute to the mother's ingenuity. She bought a light machine-made bedquilt in a department store basement for $2.95—one double bedquilt was enough for a whole chair. The quilts are real copies of old American designs and who cares if you can see the machine stitches on very close inspection!

The floor is covered with a cheery red carpet, which is actually the old dining-room carpet cut down and renovated. Red and white fringe has been added in alternate blocks—that is, about six inches of red fringe then six inches of white.

Hanging bookshelves take care of the little girl's books and her cherished collection of china animals. And a small maple desk stands between the two windows.

The bathroom, right off the bedroom, is handled very simply—dead-white walls with big red bows stenciled on them pick up the cheerful color of the bedroom carpet.

A Man's Bedroom

THIS particular gentleman is one of the many who like dark rooms for sleeping. So he has had the walls of his bedroom painted a color we call dark London fog—a dark purple gray. The floor has been covered with an allover carpet that almost exactly matches the walls. Stiff English chintz curtains with a dead-white background, green leaves and big pink and purple flowers hang at the windows. Underneath are stiff book-muslin glass curtains.

The headboard and footboard of the double bed are covered with sealing-wax-red leatherette outlined with shiny brass nails. The two straight chairs also have their seats upholstered in the same red leatherette. But the big comfortable armchair and ottoman are slip-covered in the same chintz as the curtains. The bedspread also is a quilted piece of the same chintz.

There is a big round electric clock with a shiny brass frame on the wall directly over the door. And the lamps are tall brass cylinders with specially made brass shades. (I think the lamps started life as those very high, old-fashioned brass spittoons.)

The owner of this room happens to have a hobby at which he excels --he is one of the very best amateur photographers. So he has had specially designed bookcases built along each side of the head of the bed. The tops are used for bedside tables and they are equipped with drawers of the proper size for filing film, small contact prints and his record notebooks.

On the walls he hangs giant enlargements of his pet shots, framed in wide white mats and three-inch white frames. The dark walls are a magnificent background for them.

The bathroom off this bedroom is rather original. The fixtures are black and the floor is covered with red linoleum—the same red as the head of the bed. The bathroom window has a very wide, high sill, and that has been covered with black Carrara glass. It serves as a dressing table —carries shaving cream, brush and so forth.

The walls have been painted white with a big plaid design overlaid in red and green. The shower curtain is a matching red.

12

ROOMS FOR FUN

Give Your Hobby a Home

THIRTY YEARS AGO, if an architect submitted house plans that included an adult game room his clients would have thought he had gone out of his mind. In those days even the children were shooed outside to play, and father went fishing once a year. Inside the house life was real, very earnest and definitely on the dull side.

Nowadays grownups play much more than ever before. The pulpit and the psychologists unite in urging us all to relax, develop hobbies and play games. Today you are likely to find father peacefully practicing his putting in the attic, the children screaming their way through a game of ping-pong in the cellar and mother painting a mural in the living room! Personally, I'm all for it. This desire to have our fun right at home seems to me one of the healthiest symptoms of our modern civilization.

If you have plenty of space you can have a marvelous time planning a room to fit your special interest. And even if you haven't much room there are plenty of ways to make your home more than just an attractive place of shelter.

There are so many special rooms you might want:

A library.

A general game room.

A music room.

A place for amateur theatricals.

An office.

A writing room or retreat.

A flower room or small greenhouse.

A photographic darkroom.

A carpentry room.

A gymnasium or exercise porch.

A sunroom.

Game Rooms

HERE'S A ROOM to decorate with plenty of dash: bright color combinations, sturdy, modern furniture, plenty of light and any amusing touches you care to make.

A game-room floor should certainly be very practical and tough—linoleum is ideal. And it is a poor place for fragile furniture or delicate lamps. Four steady, standing lamps—one in each corner—are probably the best idea.

A comfortable, continuous sofa that runs all along one wall is another good notion if you have some game in the center of the floor that is fun to watch.

Your game equipment will, of course, be decided by your particular preferences—a ping-pong table, a billiard table, a putting green or just a clear, polished floor for dancing. You may want a bar or a tiny kitchenette from which buffet suppers can be served. You will probably want a small radio or victrola.

On the whole, your game room will be furnished more with what you put on the walls than the furniture you use since it is really a setting for action. You can just paint the walls a lovely bright color and call it a day if you want to. Or you can treat them in some entertaining fashion—hang big, splashy travel posters (you can get them free from any big travel agency or steamship line) or perhaps hang gigantic enlargements of photographs.

A Seagoing Game Room

I KNOW ONE GAME ROOM, owned by a very nautical family, that is all decorated as if it were a ship. It is actually the remodeled boathouse of a seashore place and perches right on the water's edge.

The side of the house that faces the water is one huge sliding door opening onto a big gangplank that slopes down into the sound. Iron posts with painted white rope between them make a railing on each side of the gangplank.

The walls of the main room are of broad pine boards, unpainted. The floor is completely covered by sapphire-blue linoleum. There is a big fireplace at one end of the room and over it has been mounted a determined looking mermaid who once was the proud figurehead of an old sailing ship.

The windows are all extra-large portholes with short ship's curtains of stiff white. On the walls hang big prints of sailing ships and the room is lighted entirely by ship's lanterns.

There is a long, trestle, buffet table along one wall and a clever little galley of a kitchenette can supply steaming bowls of fish chowder on demand.

Two very wide, comfortable sofas flank the fireplace and they can both be turned into real beds when guests overflow from the main house. A ladder in one corner of the room leads the way to still more emergency sleeping quarters.

The loftlike second floor has been turned into a real dormitory for the children's guests. It is also used as the bathhouse and is equipped with two lavatories and showers and real lockers for bathing togs.

After a day on and in the water nothing could be jollier than to gather round the fireplace, sipping hot punch and singing the sea chanteys that are the specialty of the young son of the house who wields a wicked accordion for the accompaniment.

A Cellar Game Room

ANOTHER GAME ROOM I know is planned more for parties and amateur theatricals than for active sports. It is in a cellar, as are so many special rooms now that clean oil burners have made them habitable.

This particular room has solved the windowless effect of a basement very cleverly. Two full-length, fake windows have been installed in one wall on either side of the fireplace. They have real windowpanes, and in back of the glass is a space about a foot deep. On the back wall behind the glass have been pasted huge photographs of country landscape. Light bulbs, concealed along the sides, make the whole effect unbelievably convincing—I drew the curtains aside to look out of the window quite unconsciously.

The people who own this room are card fiends—they have an extra-size, permanent bridge table set up here and also a big poker table. Otherwise the room is furnished like a pleasant living room. There is one of the new tiny pianos and a radio-victrola. The sofa is flanked by end tables that are really small bookcases.

There is not too much heavy furniture in the room, however, for the center is kept clear for dancing and the rubber tiling floor is highly polished for that purpose.

At one end of the room (which is a very long oblong) is a raised platform. Heavy curtains on a pulley arrangement turn it into a tiny stage for charades or original skits. When this happens folding chairs are dragged out of a deep closet, a baby spotlight is turned on the stage and the room turns into a perfect little theater.

A Winter, Country Game Room

THIS ROOM BELONGS to a married couple I know who live in the country the year round and decided that they were tired of just holing-in and doing nothing active after the first snowfall. So they turned the room over their barn into a winter fun room.

They did the whole decorating job themselves—stained the old rafters in the peaked roof, painted the floor and put up red-and-white-checked curtains at the windows.

In the center of the room they set up a practice putting green, a ping-pong table, shuffleboard and tables for backgammon and bridge.

The room is heated by an old-fashioned pot-bellied stove. At the end of the evening the bridge tables are covered with red-and-white-checked cloths and the stove is put to use in serving refreshments.

They serve steaming hot coffee in big tin cups, hamburgers and hot dogs, coleslaw, rolls, crullers and very good ale. (The whole bill for the evening is only about $6.00.)

Every Thursday during the winter months finds them "at home" in the barn. They have competitive games and award amusing prizes, and usually their friends drop in by the dozen.

Book Rooms

MOST PEOPLE THINK of the traditional library as paneled in pine. A pine-paneled room is always lovely, of course, no matter what it is used for. But just because you can't afford real pine paneling doesn't mean that you can't achieve the same effect of snug serenity some other way.

Darkly painted walls—chocolate brown, deep green, dark navy blue, even black—all make a beautiful background for variegated book bindings. So does any color, for that matter, that doesn't compete too much with the bindings. The finest Early American libraries (the one at Mount Vernon for instance) are painted white.

If you own a large collection of books and your own house you will probably want to have your bookcases built in architecturally. Here you should certainly consult an architect who specializes in such work. You don't have to do it all at once—you can start with two cases so planned that you can add others to balance them as your books increase.

But if you live in a rented house and don't want to do anything as expensive as installing permanent bookcases there are several other things to consider. Simple, long low bookshelves can be made by any carpenter to fit any space. They are most inexpensive and as long as you keep them low enough (no more than two shelves high) they are decorative too. They are particularly useful for housing the books you keep in your living room for you can have them made just the height of your sofa arms and just as long as the sofa is deep and use them for sofa end tables. Two bookcases of this size will hold approximately one hundred books apiece.

(A timesaving way to estimate how many books you have and how much space they will require is to measure them by feet—eight books take up approximately one foot.)

Or you can buy a big break-front bookcase. Although it doesn't take up nearly as much wall space as corresponding lengths of low shelves a break-front bookcase will carry nearly four hundred books.

Whenever you have bookshelves built to order always remember to have one or two shelves built unusually deep to accommodate big books, magazines and record albums. So many ready-made bookcases make no allowance for outsize volumes.

So even though you haven't a whole room which you can turn over to your books don't hesitate to start a library if you want one. A collection of books on any subject that interests you is such a real joy to have.

Sunrooms

AMERICANS are fast turning into a nation of sun worshippers and all sorts of ingenious things are happening to the old-fashioned sun porch. If you have a sun porch nowadays you will probably want to use it all year round for one thing.

A Winter Sun Porch

I KNOW ONE SUN PORCH that is admirably equipped for winter use. It has been built onto the house in such a way that it has a fireplace back to back with the one in the living room.

The walls are all painted white, except for the outside wall opposite the fireplace. That is of great sheets of glass. They are so constructed that they can be removed entirely in the summertime, leaving just screening.

Black and white linoleum covers the floor and the ceiling is painted sky blue. The furniture is an assortment of French cane and French Provincial pieces all painted white. The comfortable chairs are slip-covered in quilted blue-and-white chintz with a touch of brilliant red, and one big sofa is all blue washable material.

There are four or five plant stands for potted plants, and white Venetian blinds can modify the light from the window wall.

The fireplace is filled with an old porcelain Dutch stove that throws out plenty of heat on crisp winter days. When the ground is covered with snow the sparkling landscape seen through the glass wall is really breathtaking. It gives you all the invigorating effect of a brisk walk across snowy fields while you are actually sitting, warm and cozy, by the pretty old stove.

An Aviary Sun Porch

ANOTHER SUN PORCH I know has a true tropical flavor. The four corners of the room have been cut off to form triangular bird cages that go all the way from the floor to the ceiling. The cages are built of bamboo and painted white. In each cage a gnarled tree trunk, with short twisted branches, has been placed and painted coral. The backs of the cage corners are deep sky blue—all the rest of the walls are white.

The bird lover who owns this room keeps her cages full of a happy, caroling variety of birds all year round.

Miscellaneous Hobby Rooms

THERE ARE SO MANY special rooms you might want that I could go on forever talking about them in detail. So I'd better start condensing right now.

You may want a tiny little office where you can have your desk and turn housekeeping into the business venture it really is.

You may want a quiet, softly lighted music room or a bare, Spartan little retreat where you can compose your soul and write the great American novel. You may want to turn that small hall bedroom over to your handy husband or son for a carpentry room. (He'll be just twice as useful if he has the equipment he longs for and a place where he can be as messy as he pleases.)

You may want a photographic darkroom. A big closet makes a fine one because you're better off without a window, anyhow, and it isn't absolutely necessary to have running water. If you can afford to have a tiny sink installed it is convenient of course. But a very small darkroom, where you can sit on a stool in the middle and reach everything you need, is much less tiring than a larger one where you stand up and walk around a lot.

You may want a sun deck instead of a sun porch—an open terrace where you can have waterproofed exercise mats and set up your rowing machine on bright days.

Hobby Closets

IF YOU CAN'T FIGURE OUT any way in which you can squeeze out a room for your hobby now's the time to haul out all your Yankee ingenuity and dust it off.

I know one man, for instance, who is an ardent amateur photographer and wanted a darkroom with all his heart. His wife insisted that there simply wasn't enough room in their three-room apartment and besides he would stain everything up with those dreadful chemicals. Finally he figured it out.

He bought one of those portable, garden tea wagons—the sort that is made of waterproof material, is set on little wheels and has two decks. His enlarger just fitted on the top deck with a little room left at one end for a pile of developing paper. His bottles of chemicals lived on the bottom deck, along with developing trays, tongs and measuring glasses. He emptied one closet in his bedroom and had special shelves built in along the sides (the closet unfortunately wasn't big enough to be the actual darkroom) to store films, paper cutter, blotters and so forth. The tea wagon just fitted into the middle of the closet when it wasn't in use, and he wheeled it neatly into the kitchen when he wanted to work. He had to wait until the dishes had been washed and put away after dinner before he could take over—but everything else about the arrangement was smooth as glass.

Just such a portable wagon could be used for painting materials if your inclinations are artistic. Then your easel and the wagon of materials could stay out of sight in a closet except when you felt like working, when the whole business could be wheeled into a corner of the living room.

A big crock of clay, covered with a damp cloth, can stand innocently in one corner of the kitchen—and that's almost all you need to have a fine time being an amateur sculptor on the kitchen table.

Whatever it is you want to do I'm certain there is a place for it some-where in your house—after all, that's what a home is for.

CASE HISTORY OF A YOUNG WOMAN IN A SHOE

Young Mrs Appletree had been married fifteen years when she realized that she certainly did have so many children she didn't know what to do. They took up so much more space than they had when they were small. There were only three of them but they just seemed to be every-where at once: in the living room listening to the loudest programs on the air every evening; in the hall trying to make electric trains go up-stairs; on the porch trying to walk the railings without breaking their necks.

She also realized that she hardly knew anyone any longer except her children. She entertained so seldom—if she did special arrangements had to be made. You couldn't send young Bobbie, aged thirteen, to bed at seven-thirty any longer. And Daphne, aged eleven, showed a decided talent for painting and had an enormous easel all over one end of the living room. When Mrs Appletree caught herself calling the grocer "Daffy" she knew the time for action had arrived.

She sacrificed the dining room completely in the cause of freedom—turned it into a game room for the young Appletrees. She kept the dining-room table but dragged it down to one end of the room and had a re-movable top made that turned it into a ping-pong table. She discarded all the rest of the dining-room furniture and substituted comfortable chairs and a sofa, all slip-covered in tough washable bath toweling.

She took up the carpet, had the floor waxed for dancing and installed a radio-victrola. One corner of the room was reserved for Daphne's studio —it is partially shielded from the rest of the room by a big screen whose inside is covered with cork. Daphne set up her easel behind the screen right by the north window and tacks her sketches on the cork screen and squints at them to her heart's content. Another corner was reserved for the baby's electric trains and mechano sets but he insists on saving space by keeping them all under the ping-pong table anyhow.

Mrs Appletree discovered a convenient flue in the wall and installed a small Franklin stove. The children have a grand time popping corn over its open fire and roasting apples on its little shelf.

Young Bobbie saved his allowance for two weeks and came home with an indoor archery set that can be set up on the ping-pong table.

You can't keep the young Appletrees—or their friends—out of their new game-living-room. Mrs Appletree happily rearranged her living room, bought a sturdy drop-leaf table for dining and plunged back into the life of a busy young matron with lots of interests and friends instead of just a harassed mother of three. After a few weeks of her new freedom she gave a party to celebrate. And she was just as surprised as the young Appletrees to discover that her party somehow flowed right into the game room and refused to be budged for the rest of the evening.

13

COOL IDEAS FOR SUMMER

Terraces, Awnings and Other Heat Waivers

I<small>F I WERE ASKED</small> to pick the loveliest day of all the year I think I would choose that very first mild day of early spring. The watery sunshine suddenly feels mellow and hot at high noon and then crisps off in cold little breezes as the afternoon wears on. Snowdrops and daffodils are recklessly showing their heads and the street vendors are hawking fat pussy willows. On that day you really believe that summer is coming again—it never seems quite possible in the middle of January! There may be several cold, dreary rainstorms after that first spring promise but they won't matter—you know what you know.

Now is the time to think about your summer plans and to map out a real campaign against the heat. Hot weather places so many of us in the same position as the shiftless man who had a leak in his roof. When the sun was shining there was no need to mend it and when it was raining he *couldn't* mend it. After real summer weather begins we are often too uncomfortably hot to do anything about cooling off! Tackle your hot weather problems now while you're still full of cool, spring energy.

187

Inside Your House in the Summer

IF YOU LIVE in a part of the country that really broils during the summer months investigate the new air-cooling units. They really do what they promise. They are not as expensive as they were a few years ago, and although they are still definitely not cheap you may find them a luxury worth having.

If you can't have air cooling place a long crystal or white porcelain tray on your window sill. In it put a block or chunks of ice covered with laurel or pine boughs and behind it place one or two electric fans. (The silent, rubber-bladed fans are most inconspicuous.) They will supply you with a surprisingly arctic breeze. And if you happen to have a potted fern or two place them in front of your iceberg. The fan will blow their fronds about in tropical style.

Open your windows and hoist your Venetian blinds only after the sun has set. Southern houses have been kept reasonably cool in this simple way for generations.

A bucket exhaust fan in the window will do wonders for your kitchen.

Don't have too many lights burning at night. Every light gives out heat as well as light. Candles give out a certain amount of heat but not as much.

Get rid of any clutter. Remove everything you can possibly spare from each room and leave only enough to keep it from resembling a barn. (You'll probably get to like the spacious effect so much that you'll end the summer wondering how you ever stood so much junk around.)

If you don't like entirely bare floors put down white string carpet, or fiber, or matting.

Take down the curtains. If you think the windows too bare hang curtains of crisp, white book muslin or colored mosquito netting, tied back with great bunches of field flowers. Or use a stiff, shaped valance—either painted or covered with fabric—which continues down the sides of the windows and so frames the opening but leaves the windows themselves free to admit every little breeze. If you have two windows at one end of a room curtain them as one with the inside frames bare.

Cover all the upholstered furniture with cool, washable slip covers. (They needn't be expensive material just as long as they are slick and easily laundered.)

If your bed is draped substitute white book muslin and have a counterpane to match. Do the same for your dressing table if it's skirted.

Whitewash the inside of the fireplace. Either keep a fire laid, with a crisp white paper fan underneath it (and fine guests a quarter for shooting cigarette stubs into it), or keep your fireplace filled with fresh green laurel or pine.

If you intend to repaint or repaper in the autumn you may even want to whitewash one end of your living room for the summer.

Change your colored lamp shades for pleated white paper ones or stiff white buckram. You can give any lamp base a coat of flat white cold-water paint.

After your house looks as cool as a dell begin telling your friends (this has nothing to do with decorating but I guarantee it) that you're so fortunate because you don't feel the heat. By August you'll probably believe it.

Outside Your House in the Summer

ONCE YOU HAVE SETTLED the matter of summer clothes for the inside of your house the chances are very high that you will start some sort of outdoor planning, for Americans are learning to use the out-of-doors

TABLE SET FROM THE FIVE-AND-TEN-CENT STORE
Style Without Money

THE PROBLEM   To substitute good taste for money in such a way that charm will not suffer in the least and money will be saved for other more important expenditures.

THE SOLUTION   Just to prove that it could be done this dinner table was set with articles bought exclusively in the five-and-ten-cent store, including the cloth.

1. The cloth and napkins are of white organdy with green dots, bought by the yard and hemmed at home.

2. The china is a fresh lettuce green.

3. The knives and forks have Chinese-red composition handles (very effective).

4. The cigarette containers are entertaining—high hats made of glass.

5. The flower vases are an unusually graceful design—filled with red tulips.

6. Although the curtains behind the table did not come from the five-and-ten-cent store they are not at all expensive. The glass curtains are simple white muslin—the sort that can be bought, all made up, in any good department store. The over curtains are of brilliant Irish green taffeta so simply draped that they could be made at home by any enterprising bride.

7. The chairs have Queen Anne legs, but they have been amusingly pulled into the Victorian era by the heavy tufting. They are covered in magenta satin.

more and more each year. The growing custom of spending winters in the South has taught us how to spend summers in the North to much better advantage.

Perhaps you will cross the living room, throw up the window and decide on new awnings or new window boxes this year. Perhaps you will step out onto your little balcony or terrace and remodel it in your mind. Perhaps you will walk through your garden and brood about all sorts of new plantings later on.

Strangely enough this back-to-the-soil movement is strongest in the big cities. New Yorkers, in particular, have gone slightly mad on the subject of terraces, penthouses and backyard gardens. They have suddenly remembered that houses have roofs, even in a city of concrete and steel. Tiny gardens and outdoor living rooms have blossomed all over the city. Landlords who are fortunate enough to be able to claim ten square feet of back yard or a minute balcony boost the rent of the apartment exactly as much as if it had an additional room. And that is exactly what it is, if cleverly used—an extra, outdoor room.

If country folk only knew how fiercely a New Yorker cherishes her handkerchief-size terrace they would make much better use of their own generous grounds. There's something about human nature that makes us undervalue what's under our noses. But when the out-of-doors is reduced to a matter of feet and inches, instead of acres, that's when we all realize that no ceiling can possibly be as thrilling as the sky, no wallpaper as lovely as serried greenery and the most expensive carpet in the world can't be as restful to the feet as just plain grass.

So the city dweller gets every possible ounce of satisfaction out of her porch or garden. She has her breakfast and her dinner there as often as possible. She entertains there, does her exercises and even sleeps under the stars on breathless nights. She has to fight a relentless battle against soot and she has to use her wits to provide any sort of privacy on her terrace or roof. But she has found that it's well worth it.

I agree with her heartily. There is something gay and dramatic about eating out-of-doors, especially at night. The architecture that has grown in Florida and California has shown us the romance of the patio way of living. The very word—patio—makes one think of fragrant bougain-villea vines, mimosa trees and flaming red hibiscus.

If you live in the country all that romance is yours for the taking. If you live in town you can find it on the smallest terrace or balcony.

Naturally, you must plan your out-of-doors living with real care. You can't slap a few deck chairs out on the lawn and then expect to spend the summer there. You won't do it because you won't be nearly comfortable enough. Furnishing and arranging your balcony, terrace or garden is exactly like arranging another living room. Awnings, furniture, equipment for eating, must all be selected thoughtfully.

Awnings

ON A CITY TERRACE a big awning is almost an essential—both for the sake of privacy and as a defense against soot. And even in the country an awning seems to pull your outdoor group together pleasantly and give a sense of privacy.

Unfortunately, awnings are definitely not cheap. New ones are very expensive and the upkeep is high also. It is a real necessity to keep your awnings immaculate, however. They will instantly tear down your whole effect of cool comfort if they are shabby or dirty. (If your awning has seen its best days try painting the whole thing with fresh paint. You won't be able to roll it up and down any longer but it will look like new just as often as you repaint it.)

Another inexpensive dodge is to use bamboo shades (the sort that are sometimes substituted for Venetian blinds) instead of real awnings. They can be strung up with some sort of pulley arrangement or just stretched flat on a simple wood frame. Then you can paint them any color you want and as often as you want. They won't shut out all the sunshine, of course, but they will modify it and sift it down in effective slanting streaks.

If you are buying real awnings select the colors with your mind on the thermometer—keep them as cool as possible. There has been an unfortunate fad for lots of orange in awnings lately. At least I think it is unfortunate for I consider orange just about the hottest color there is. Strangely enough, plain bright red (if the red is trimmed and lined with white) seems much cooler than orange.

White, of course, is supreme in the summertime. Since plain white awnings aren't very practical, however, just be sure you mix your other color with lots of white trimmings.

Soft blue, lined with white and fringed with white, makes a delightful awning.

So does dark blue trimmed with white.

Or emerald green and white stripes. (The stripes should be extra wide —8 inches.)

Or red and white stripes, lined and fringed with white.

But to my mind the very coolest combination of all is an awning of pale lemon-yellow, lined with white and fringed with white cotton.

Outdoor Furniture

THE MOST DURABLE outdoor furniture is that made of painted cast iron. It is more expensive than other varieties though and isn't nearly as comfortable. Also, it is so heavy that dragging it around is a real job. Reed, rattan or the wooden chairs with sloping backs (sometimes called Adirondack chairs) are all more comfortable. These wooden chairs will last a reasonable number of years even if left outside. They can all be equipped with soft, removable cushions that can be taken in at night.

If I were working on a very limited budget for my porch or terrace furniture I know just where I would splurge. I would blow myself to one of those heavenly comfortable, double chaise longues. They have downy, removable cushions, adjustable backs and big hoods. And they are set on wheels so that they can follow the sun around easily.

Add several inexpensive canvas deck chairs to the big chaise longue and you will have a very good nucleus for any garden group.

But don't stop there! An outdoor group should be arranged exactly as a living-room group. To be really comfortable you will need several end tables, just the height of the chair arms, and possibly a low coffee table for ash trays and magazines, a thermos bottle of water or a tray of lemonade.

And if you really plan to live out-of-doors as much as possible you will want some sort of lighting. You can install waterproof lanterns for permanent light and use candles in hurricane shades for dining. Or you can use a baby spotlight, concealed in shrubbery and focused on your garden group. I think the use of a baby spot is by far the most dramatic—it makes the whole scene look like a romantic stage-set.

A light exercise mat that can be thrown down on the grass is another useful addition to out-of-doors furniture. So are waterproofed beach rolls and odd cushions for grass sitters.

If you live in the country and are fortunate enough to have a swimming pool by all means arrange outdoor chairs and tables on its brink. So many pools are just great tubs of water where you swim, idle just a minute on hard concrete or prickly grass and then go back to the house. A few wooden chairs (the sort made of slats so that you can sit in them and drip through), a few beach rolls, and a table for cool drinks or cigarettes would make them so much more tempting.

If you like out-of-doors eating dig up some sort of buffet table. If you don't want to buy a cast-iron one with a glass top use an old kitchen table, freshly painted and with its top covered in gay new oilcloth. A big food heater is a boon for outdoor meals (I think there should always be one hot dish no matter what the thermometer says). Dress up your outdoor meals in party style—use cheerful peasant ware, big wooden bowls of salad, lobster-red cooking pots, big pottery bowls of fruit. A flock of painted trays will simplify your service problem. You might paint the trays the same bright red as your cooking pots and then let everyone help himself from the buffet table.

I think outdoor entertaining is the best of all—you can accommodate such hoards of people at such small expense and the atmosphere can be so informal and hearty.

Outdoor Color Schemes

FOLLOW THE SUGGESTIONS about awnings here—keep everything very cool and simple. Use plenty of white. (I think that white is always tremendously important decoratively, but in the summer it is unbeatable.)

Whatever colors you select be sure your plan is unified. Avoid striped effects that jumble five or six hot colors. If you have selected a pale blue awning with white fringe you might paint all your wooden furniture white and use blue cushions. Or you might want to use red and white cushions on the blue furniture to give a note of sharp contrast.

In general I think it is only practical to paint all the wooden outdoor furniture the same color. It will all have to be done again next spring and one color is just that much cheaper and less trouble.

If your outdoor room is close to the living room it is often a good idea to continue the living-room colors—pull your living room right out onto the lawn.

Your Growing Background

IF YOU HAVE A GARDEN as a background for your outdoor living room you are so lucky that you shouldn't need a word of advice from me. But to the eternal astonishment of the city dweller, who has to use brains and money every minute to provide the illusion of more land and more growing things than she really has, her out-of-town friend often makes very poor use of her lovely surroundings.

Of course there are exceptions, but this failure to use the out-of-doors when it is all about us is so common that it bears a little thinking about. I believe I know the answer. The city dweller, because she lives in a highly congested area, is *forced* to provide herself at the very beginning with one all-important factor—privacy. The first thing she does when she furnishes a terrace is to devise some system of awnings, potted shrubs or blinds to protect her from the surrounding windows. The country dweller is not nearly as badly off to start with and so she frequently does nothing about it at all.

Suburban houses actually have no more privacy than city terraces. Even houses in the real country often face main roads and are very close to them. On very big estates the swimming pool is often too near the house itself or the dining terrace fronts the main driveway.

So, before you lucky country dwellers do any outdoor furniture shopping at all I advise you to shop like mad for the greatest essential—a sense of seclusion and privacy.

Sometimes a hedge will give it to you, or a planting of trees and shrubs, or an arbor over which vines can be trained. Sometimes you need a wall of brick, stone, cement or woven wood, depending on the nature of your property. Sometimes an overhead trellis for vines or a big awning will be all you need to cut those second-story windows next door right out of the picture.

After you have created an outdoor room that you don't have to share with the entire countryside—that is entirely your own—you can go hog-wild as far as a flowery background is concerned.

But if you are a terrace gardener you will probably have to get your effects from potted plants and shrubs. Here are a few growing things which I have discovered will survive the city climate with fair success:

Privet hedge—this will grow as high as 15 feet in a city garden.

Rhododendron or laurel bushes.

Rose of Sharon.

Syringa bushes.

Wisteria and trumpet vines.

Ailanthus, South Carolina poplar and willow trees.

English ivy—either climbing or rambling over the ground instead of grass.

All bulbs—daffodils, narcissus, iris, begonias.

If you have a terrace rather than a backyard garden your small trees and shrubs will have to live in big tubs. (Butter tubs, coaxed from your grocer and painted, are fine.) Do study the arrangement of such tubs so that you will get the most balanced, established look possible. The Italians are particularly clever at arranging potted shrubs and bushes. Get hold of some photographs of Italian gardens if you can and study their lovely formal designs.

Bulbs do fairly well on city terraces or in city gardens. And rows of potted, flowering plants are usually a neater, easier solution of the flower problem than is fussing around with seedlings. The soot, the driving rains of summer thunderstorms, the brazen sun—are all against your poor seedlings. And potted plants can be replaced at very little expense.

A city terrace is no place for tangled wildwood effects anyhow. Half its effect depends on a sparkling neatness—every dead leaf should be pinched off, every pot tidy. It is much easier to keep your terrace fresh as a daisy with rows of potted flowers than with flats of struggling shoots.

CASE HISTORY OF A CITY OASIS

When young Mrs Maple discovered that Mr Maple's business was going to keep them tied to New York all summer she was so disappointed that she threw a mild fit of hysterics. She had only spent one summer in town in her life and she had grim memories of a sticky, stifling hotel room where she had been so unbearably hot that she had longed to melt completely away and never harden into life again.

When she calmed down Mr Maple said he was sorry in such a worried way that she bucked up and smiled wanly at him. They made a few feeble week-end plans during April and then decided to count on invitations from out-of-town friends.

But one warm May day Mrs Maple felt energetic. She opened the back window of their apartment and climbed out onto the rather grubby extension roof there. It didn't look like much. It was just twenty feet long by about twelve feet deep and was enclosed by a rusty iron railing. Everything was gritty with thick city dust.

When you looked away from the roof, though, the effect was exhilarating. The apartment houses across the way were made of that pinkish stone used so much in New York, and they looked actually lovely against the blue spring sky. Over one roof in the distance a great flock of pigeons dipped and circled.

The woman directly across the way was busily hosing down her little roof garden, while a wildly excited wire-haired terrier barked and snapped at the hose. Mrs Maple watched her wistfully for a few moments. Then her wistful look was replaced by one of surprised determination. She didn't have a jolly little dog, but she certainly had a roof that was at least two and one half feet bigger than that one over there. She slapped on her hat and headed for the nearest hardware store for a hose. And though she didn't realize it, from that moment on there was no turning back—she was a confirmed terrace hound!

The Maple roof was the scene of hectic activity for the next two weeks. Two little stile steps on each side of the window made running in and out easier. The floor of the roof was painted black and the iron railing white. The terrace was protected on two sides by brick walls—the wall of the Maples' own house and the wall of the house next door. Both these walls were also painted white and a big red-and-white striped awning stretched over the whole terrace.

In the center of the long, solid brick wall Mrs Maple hung a big white plaster plaque. (Mr Maple had found it in a junk shop.) The plaque was about four feet long and was a lovely copy of an archaic Greek frieze. The plaque was flanked on either side by tall, slender ladders, painted white and fastened flush against the wall. Semicircular tubs were placed at the foot of each ladder and ivy was trained up them. Directly under the plaque Mrs Maple placed her long buffet table.

Since she intended to use her terrace until it screamed for help she bought a big plate warmer for the center of the buffet table. (These warmers come in a variety of styles—some have alcohol lamps, some electric heating units and the least expensive have three big Sterno cans.)

She also bought some white deck chairs with red-and-white canvas backs and several outdoor tables. She placed big white pots of geraniums in a stiff row along the railing, and she always keeps big glass vases of apple blossoms or lilacs or cut flowers at each end of her buffet table just as if it were an indoor living room. In the evening the terrace is lighted by tall white candles in hurricane glass chimneys.

A candlelit evening on the Maple terrace, sipping iced drinks and talking quietly over the dimmed strains of the small portable radio, is the perfect end to an imperfect hot day.

CASE HISTORY OF A SATURDAY-NIGHT HOUSE

Mr and Mrs Goodfellow are a young couple with all the spirit in the world. They love to be out-of-doors, they love games and they love company. Unfortunately, their income doesn't nearly match their energy. The first year they were married they discovered that after they had paid for a pleasant apartment in town there wasn't much left over for the very things they loved best. When summer came around they were pretty doleful for they certainly didn't have enough money for the week-end country cottage they longed for. They got quite a few week-end invitations but they were basically the sort of people who would much rather be hosts than guests so they didn't have a really good time.

The next year Mrs Goodfellow suggested an experiment. They took a smaller and much cheaper apartment in town which cut down their entertaining even further. But they took a flier and bought a country place. At first they were ashamed to call it a "country place"—for it was really just an old hay barn. They got it for practically nothing because it was in such unattractive condition. You could actually see sky through the chinks in the walls. The former owner had started to remodel it as a sort of playhouse or guest house. He had taken out the stalls and haymow and so turned it into one enormous room. He had also installed a kitchen alcove and one bath. Still, it wasn't a very promising building and Mr Goodfellow only succumbed when he saw the lively little brook in back of the house and tested the depth of the swimming hole with a long stick.

The first thing they did was the most expensive—they had another large bath installed and had three very roomy closets built into each bathroom. They also had one huge closet—almost a room—built into one corner of the big main room.

The chinks in the walls were filled in, and since the roof was tight, that was that. They left the walls their natural color and painted the floor deep bright blue. Since the beams of the ceiling were not hand-hewn nor particularly interesting in their natural state they painted them blue also.

Then Mrs Goodfellow bought two large, comfortable sofas and covered them in rough-textured, clear red homespun. She also bought six good box springs and mattresses.

Mr Goodfellow looked at the six beds sitting in the middle of the only room and asked nervously, "A dormitory?"

"Go away and play golf," answered Mrs Goodfellow soothingly, and sent for the local carpenter.

She had him build double-decker bunks on either side of the big fireplace and two single bunks opposite it. The bunks each had a window in back of them and could be closed off from the room by folding shutter doors. In the daytime the beds were turned into sofas. At night, after the shutters were closed, they were perfectly private little berths. They were a great deal more private than Pullman berths, as a matter of fact, because the shutters were wooden. And they were much more comfortable because they were larger. Each bunk had its own good reading lamp and hanging bookshelf on the wall.

The rest of the decoration went like lightning. Mrs Goodfellow made a trip to a country auction and bought all sorts of wood furniture—chests, small tables and chairs of every description and a huge trestle table for eating. Then she painted them all blue and stenciled bright, stiff little bunches of flowers on the chest drawers and the backs of the chairs.

A few black-and-white, oblong, cowhide rugs scattered here and there on the blue floor gave an amusing new touch.

She painted the frames of the windows white and placed rows of potted geraniums on the broad sills. She bought simple, inexpensive, big lamps and tall white candles for the trestle dining table.

When she was finished she had a real Hansel and Gretel house. But Mr Goodfellow was still worrying about the sleeping arrangements.

"A dormitory," he said determinedly.

"Well, suppose it *is*," cried Mrs Goodfellow. "When people come to the country they *want* something crazy and informal. Let's invite the Smiths and the Browns next week end and just see what happens."

They had a hilarious week end. And it was astonishingly comfortable. One bathroom was turned over to the men, the other to the women. Both bathrooms were big enough to serve as dressing rooms—the closets were roomy, and Mrs Goodfellow had equipped them with chests of drawers and dressing tables. The big closet in the main room was used for sports litter—golf bags, tennis rackets, suitcases—and so kept the big room tidy.

When all the shutters were closed at night Mr Goodfellow admitted (from the upper bunk) that he felt completely secluded. And the next morning Mr Brown, who had read quietly in his bunk till all hours, slept long after the rest of the crowd got up and never even heard their cheerful clatter as they got breakfast at the other end of the huge room.

People fight for week-end invitations from the Goodfellows. And even though Mr Goodfellow is still shaking his head over the bunks I think Mrs Goodfellow knew what she was about from the very beginning. When people go to the country they want to relax. And it's much easier to let go in a real playhouse—where everything is entirely different from life at home. You can take a chicken coop and get more pleasure out of it than a marble palace—just as long as you do it with an air!

Dining-Room Equipment

1. Dining table, chairs, serving table and sideboard—only if you intend to have a real dining room.

2. A firm, drop-leaf table for living-room dining.

3. China. (Try to get plenty of some open stock pattern—enough for a reserve supply.)

4. Glass. (Get a reserve here, too, if you can.)

5. Tablecloths and napkins.

6. Tea cloths and napkins.

7. Cocktail napkins, either cloth or specially initialed paper ones.

8. Doilies and lunch mats.

9. A breakfast tray, with special linen and china.

10. Four candlesticks—silver, glass or plated.

11. Four candy or nut dishes.

12. Two or three centerpieces—lovely bowls or covered silver soup tureens.

13. Tea set—silver, plated or china.

14. After-dinner coffee set.

15. Nutcrackers and picks.

16. Big wooden salad bowl.

17. Flat silver.

18.

19.

20.

21.

22.

23.

Bedroom

1. A bed, or twin beds.
2. Two bedside end tables.
3. Two straight chairs.
4. A chaise longue, or comfortable chair and ottoman.
5. Two chests of drawers.
6. A pair of large lamps.
7. Two reading bed lamps.
8. A low table for the chaise longue.
9. A dressing table. (Only if you have room and really want one.)
10. Blankets—two weights.
11. Linen. (Get just as much linen and blankets as you possibly can. Amazing as it may seem now there may be babies later on and you'll thank goodness for a reserve supply.)
12. Two quilts.
13. Two particularly handsome comforters.
14. Closet equipment: hat stands, hangers, clothing bags and so forth.
15. Bathroom accessories: a scale, clothes hamper, shower curtain and bathroom linen.
16.
17.
18.
19.
20.
21.

Kitchen

1. A complete set of cooking utensils. (This may seem like a prosaic present but it is a joy to have the very best equipment available, and it is definitely not cheap.)
2.
3.
4.

Miscellaneous and Luxuries

1. A warm rug for your car.
2. A fitted dressing case.
3. A camera.
4. A handsome food heater for buffet parties.
5. Other buffet equipment.
6. A picnic basket.
7. A bedside clock.
8. A bedside thermos pitcher.
9. Two small radios—one for bedroom, one for kitchen.
10. A pair of hanging bookshelves.
11. A Servidor for the bathroom door.
12. A cedar chest.
13. A piano.
14. A radio-victrola.
15. A bird cage or aquarium.
16. Any personal luxury that you've always wanted and will never get around to buying for yourself.
17.
18.

Naturally, this list will need plenty of revising before it fits your particular case. You will undoubtedly subtract from it and add to it. I have really included it here just to start you thinking about your own list, and possibly to give you a few suggestions that will be new to you.

The important thing is to make such a list—and to use it. Tame those wild wedding presents and make them really help you. For this is your only chance. Even if you get married six more times you can never expect such bounty again.

That Little Matter of a Budget

YOUR LIST will help you budget your money for furnishing and decorating, too. If you have organized all the things you need you can easily figure just how thin to spread the butter on the bread.

I think it would be silly for me to attempt to give you the exact sums you should spend on various items because they will vary so enormously with the total sum you have. One thing I can tell you, however. A whole apartment can be completely furnished for much, much less than you dream.

Just by way of example, one big New York department store has set up three charmingly arranged apartments right in the store. The cost of each one is well under a thousand dollars. And those apartments are complete, even to Belgian Lourd glasses on the dining table and gay dish towels in the kitchen.

That, of course, is the lazy way to go about it—every single thing in those model apartments is available in the average large department store, and you have to pay retail prices. You could create exactly as charming an apartment with a quarter or even a tenth of that money if you used plenty of imagination and ingenuity. Persistent visits to auction rooms, shrewd buying in the secondhand stores and the rejuvenation of hand-me-downs would shrink your total cost so that you'd never recognize it.

The trick is to plan your expenditures shrewdly—splurge where it does the most good and pinch pennies where you'll never notice the difference. In one inexpensive apartment, for instance, all the wood furniture could start out as cheap unfinished pine. Then it could be stained or painted to suit the decorative scheme of each room.

In general, here are the things on which I think you can economize, and the things on which I think you should spend:

Save on:

Carpets or rugs.

All wooden furniture. (You have plenty of time for antiques or solid mahogany later on.)

Curtains. (Yards and yards of inexpensive material in a good color will be just as effective.)

Pictures. (Really beautiful prints are very inexpensive today and if smartly framed will answer every purpose.)

Spend on:

Upholstered furniture.

Beds.

Lamps.

All accessories.

Linen.

Silver. (Keep it down to a minimum but make that minimum very good.)

Furniture Arrangement

SINCE you will be installing completely new furniture in a completely new apartment, you will help yourself enormously if you make a little picture of each room. You don't have to be a draughtsman at all. Just go to the nearest stationery store and buy ten cents worth of paper that has been all ruled off in little squares of ordinary graph paper.

Then measure the dimensions of your room. You can use an ordinary tape measure but if you want to make things easy for yourself get a surveyor's tape. It's fifty feet long and you won't have to put it down and then shove it along as you will a five-foot tape measure.

Once you have discovered that your room is, say, 16 feet wide, 20 feet long and 12 feet high, call each little square on the paper one foot and draw an exact replica of the shape of your room. Run the walls out on each side just as if the room were a paper box which you have slit down each corner and flattened out. Measure the doors, windows, fireplace and radiators and draw them in on your walls.

Now you can snip out the furniture sketched on the next two pages and shove it around in your paper house until you hit upon just the arrangement you want. You may find that you don't need nearly as much as you thought you did. Or you may find that the particular living room into which you are moving actually cries out for something you had not counted on at all. One thing I believe you will discover for certain—you can always get more upholstered furniture into a room than you expect at first. (That's why I included two sofas in my list of living-room essentials—you probably thought I was being overgenerous.)

Whatever happens, this grown-up version of cutting out paper dolls is a wonderful game for it will help you plan your house as a whole. And after you have done that the battle is half won.

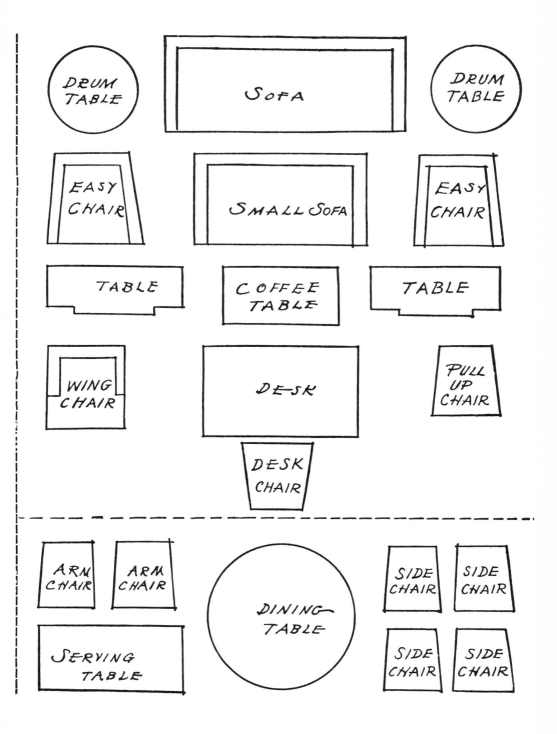

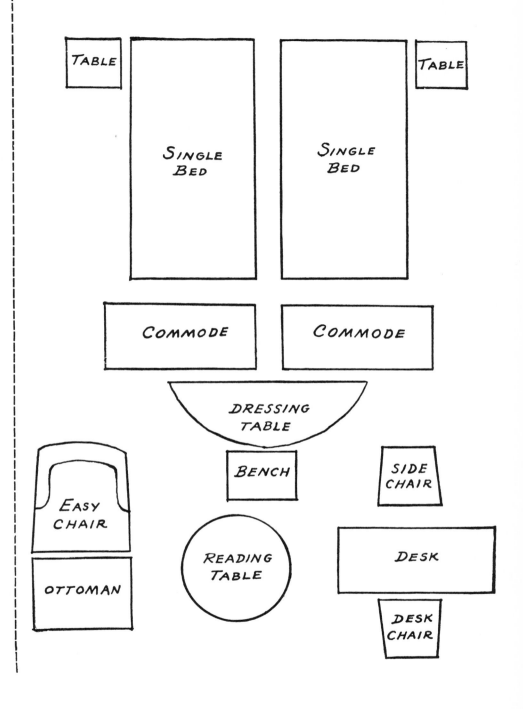

Your Decorative Scheme as a Whole

YOU'RE PROBABLY fairly bursting with your own confident plans about the actual details of your decoration. If, however, you do happen to get panicky, always remember that you can consult some decorator you trust without involving yourself in a complete decorative service. Twenty-five dollars spent on a personal interview is often money well invested. It will crystallize your own ideas and help you over the bumps.

15

BEFORE YOU BUILD

How to Get the House You Want

THE DAY on which you decide that the time has come to build your own house is probably one of the most thrilling in your whole life.

Before you reach the delirious planning stage you have undoubtedly thought and dreamed a lot about the house you want. This sort of dreaming is very important. The successful house is usually one that has been finished and torn down again many, many times inside someone's head. If you plan to build five years from now it's not too soon to start lining up your ideas.

Look at magazine pictures and plans of houses, cut them out and start a scrapbook. Take a snapshot of any house you run across that appeals to you. When you are on a trip or a vacation look about you for houses you like. You may find just the house you would love to own—or just the type of house which you know would make you happy. You needn't be afraid that you won't recognize it—it will look like an old friend. Before you take the final, decisive step you should have a solid, satisfying knowledge of what you really want.

You will need that knowledge. For between you and your dream house stands a man—your architect. You can't expect him to do the perfect job of which he is capable unless you are prepared to contribute your most intelligent co-operation.

I strongly advise against attempting to build without this very important fellow. I built three houses for myself before I became a decorator, two with architects and one without. The one built without an architect was by far the most expensive in the end. A good architect will save your money and insure your success.

Choosing Your Architect

THIS is not something to be undertaken lightly—it is the most important single step you'll make. *Don't* go to the first architect whom you find charming at dinner. *Don't* go to the attractive young man who went to college with a friend of a friend of your brother-in-law merely because he seems so sympathetic and practical. Your architect should never be chosen on anything less than complete knowledge of his ability. For your house will never be any better than the man who carries it through.

Find out critically the exact man for the particular style of architecture you want. That attractive young man you met last week may specialize in banks for all you know. Every architect has his own special taste and has usually made a success in one particular type of house. If the house you want isn't in his line he may accept your job but his heart won't be in it. If he knows in advance that you and he think alike about houses you're off to a fine start.

If you don't know just where to find your architect watch the good magazines for pictures of houses you like. Then write in to the editor and ask for the name and address of the man who designed them. There is no end to the satisfaction a really good architect can give you. Aside from saving you money he will undoubtedly contribute new and exciting ideas of his own. And he will know all about the latest building and zoning regulations, requirements of the fire laws, the best of the new materials.

If you plan to have a decorator or a landscape architect don't wait until later on to find them. They should be selected right along with your architect so that all three can consult from the very beginning.

When you're building a house it definitely pays to make the whole job just as close to perfection as you can possibly manage. There is no bulkier white elephant than a mediocre house if you ever want to sell. On the other hand, an unusual, distinguished house—even though it have only four rooms—will always have a resale or rental value.

What Sort of House Do You Really Want?

EVEN THOUGH you've selected the best architect in the world you can't expect him to be a mindreader. That's why I said before that you will need a very solid knowledge of just what you want in order to work intelligently with him. I know from my own experience that it is rarely the architect's fault when a client doesn't get what she wants.

When I built my first house I was totally inexperienced and made many mistakes that I would not make today. But I think they were average mistakes. When the plans were all finished I remember suddenly wondering why on earth I hadn't mentioned the little lean-to greenhouse opening off the living room that I had always longed for. And why I had forgotten to tell the architect that the dumbwaiter should go all the way from the kitchen to the top floor because I intended to use that for a nursery. And why I hadn't had concrete partitions laid out in the cellar to accommodate a future oil burner. It is incredible the important things you are likely to forget in all the excitement of blueprints and diagrams!

So do prepare yourself thoroughly for your conferences with your architect. Both architects and decorators are only human, and they both face the supreme task of getting inside their clients' minds. It is often necessary to be absurdly confidential with them about just the sort of life your family leads, your personal idiosyncrasies, your habits. Otherwise they can't possibly hope to give you a comfortable place in which to live a life about which they know nothing.

In order to help you organize your requirements I've prepared a sort of rambling questionnaire which attempts to take up all those questions your architect will have to ask you.

What Type of House

WHAT period or style of house do you like best?

I have put this question first because it is usually asked first. Actually, I think it is often a better idea to decide about the inside of your house before the outside. In this way you will analyze the sort of house you need by the sort of life you lead, and the outside style will really frame itself about your living.

Even though it is unnecessary for interior decoration to follow rigidly the style of architecture, still the same general atmosphere will probably prevail. So instead of thinking of a strict Georgian house, or strict French Provincial, think of what general quality you prefer. If you like balanced, formal rooms—almost classical in their serenity—you may want a Georgian or Southern American house. (Beautiful examples of this type of architecture can be found in Charleston or along the James River in Virginia.) A Regency house might suit you too.

If you like a more informal, rambling, romantic house you will probably fit into an Early Colonial, French Provincial or English Tudor sort of place. The famous House of the Seven Gables or the lovely, sprawling houses in Williamsburg all go in this category.

Or perhaps you are all in favor of the twentieth century, and want to be completely modern. The countryside is dotted with excellent little model homes that will give you loads of suggestions for this style of living.

When you're deciding about style remember also to consider its suitability to your locality. You may want what you want no matter where you're going to build it, but it's always wise to think of resale possibilities.

Size

How BIG A HOUSE do you want? The modern trend is all toward smaller, more efficient houses than were built ten years ago. If you need, or love, a big house consider copying one of the beautiful eighteenth-century American houses. They were designed with a central, main house and two wings on each side. The wings can be connected with the main house by arcades which can be shut off completely if you ever want to cut down expenses, or after the children grow up and marry.

If you are young, think of the future and have your house so designed that additions can be made later on.

Building Materials

CERTAIN building materials are more or less implied by certain architectural styles, and this is a matter to take up in detail with your architect. There are so many to consider that I'll just mention a few:

Clapboard

Shingle

Shiplap

Brick—plastered or whitewashed

Stone—possibly whitewashed too

Half timber

You have a wide choice of roofs, too. They can be shingle, slate, seamed tin, composition or any one of a half dozen other possibilities. Here's where your architect's expert advice is invaluable.

But here's one thing you should check on yourself, before you set your heart on any particular material. Costs vary widely in different localities. Find out which materials are available, and therefore reasonable, in your particular neighborhood.

The Vestibule

YOU NEEDN'T HAVE ONE if you don't want to—but it offers welcome protection in bad weather and reduces the cleaning problem. If you do decide on a vestibule, remember that this is the first impression your house has to offer. So many vestibules are characterless boxes. Strike your first note of beautiful formality, or gay charm and hospitality, right here. A floor of brick, marble, tile, zenitherm or any easily washed material is better than wood. So why not have a floor specially designed for the vestibule? Consider special wall treatment and lighting, too.

Entrance Hall

Do YOU WANT THIS to be a mere passage or a real room? Have you ever considered an entrance hall with a fireplace in it? Or one with a big bay window for plants? In any case, plan on two large coat closets and consider adding a dressing room and lavatory. Or, if yours is an active family, how about an extra-large closet room for golf clubs, tennis rackets, sleds, skis and so forth. This sports closet might have direct access to the out-of-doors.

Living Room

How BIG do you want this room to be and of what general shape? Do you want it to be informal in character—irregular in shape and with a low ceiling? Or do you want a more formal room with simple, classical proportions and a high ceiling? Unless you live in an extreme climate you must decide on the best direction for this room to face for maximum coolness in summer and maximum sun in winter. Have you considered the possibility of having wide floor boards instead of the usual narrow parquet boards? Or thought whether this might not be a good place to save money on the flooring, and carpet to the walls? (If you are remodeling an old house with bad floors, check on the cost of covering all floors with good black linoleum in place of a repair job.) Do you want a fireplace? Do you entertain many people? If you do, plan to make it possible to throw the living room and an adjoining room together for parties. Do you want bookcases? If so, they should be planned now. Have you any specially big pieces of furniture? If you have, the wall space must be laid out accordingly.

Book Room, Game Room, Hobby Room

IF YOU WANT A LIBRARY do you want to investigate the cost of pine paneling? Do you want a fireplace? Do you want to plan the library with the view in mind, and perhaps with access to the out-of-doors?

Do you want a real game room, built right into the house? Do you want a hobby room—or a room that can be turned into a hobby room at some future date?

Dining Room

Is THIS THE PLACE where you may be able to save space and do without a proper dining room? If you must have one, how big should it be? What do you visualize in it—a fireplace—a bay window for the breakfast table —niches in which you can display china? Plan your dining-room lighting as you plan the room if you intend to use wall brackets. How about access to a dining terrace for summertime?

Pantry

MANY MODERN HOUSES are built without pantries but this means an open kitchen door when food is brought in, and a much more crowded kitchen. If you do want a pantry, reserve space for a large plate warmer and have plenty of electric outlets, as well as a sink and ample cupboards.

Kitchen

DO YOU LIKE TO HAVE breakfast in the kitchen? Or do your servants eat there? If so, be sure the room is large enough and consider installing an attractive dining alcove for kitchen meals. Try to decide on the equipment you intend to use—refrigerator, stove, sink, possible laundry tubs. If you can make a floor plan of your equipment you will be sure of getting an efficient kitchen. Do you want to allow for some sort of forced-draft ventilation?

Laundry

DO YOU WANT ONE, or do you intend to use tubs in the kitchen? If you do intend to have a real laundry investigate special electrical equipment, ventilation, accessibility to your drying yard and the possibility of a laundry chute from upstairs.

Halls

SINCE halls are scantily furnished their proportion, trim, floor and wall finish must all be as interesting as possible. Have you any special ideas on trim? Would you like to line some halls with shelves, or cupboards with shutter doors? How about having the upstairs hall open onto a flat roof that can be used as a sun deck?

Stairways

MANY SMALLER HOUSES nowadays omit a back stairway. But remember that if you do this everything and everybody must go up and down your front stairs—furniture when moved, workmen, children and servants. Having just one stairway robs you of a certain amount of privacy.

Do you want to make your front stairs important? If you do, collect pictures of beautiful curving stairs or lovely balustrades until you find just what you want. If you have an elderly person in your family how about installing an inexpensive lift?

Bedrooms

How MANY BEDROOMS do you need in all for family, guests, servants? Do you want certain exposures for the morning sun, or lack of it? Do you want fireplaces in certain bedrooms? Do you want windows to the floor? Do you want terraces or balconies opening off your bedrooms or a big bath-dressing-room for yourself? Have you planned plenty of outlets for special bedside lighting, for your sun lamp and for your heating pad? Have you really allowed plenty of closet space? How about a small closet in each bedroom to house the linen and blankets for that particular room?

Bathrooms

Do you need a bath for each bedroom or one between two? Do you want them tiled or mirrored or do you intend to paint or paper? How about the floor coverings—tile, cork, rubber tiling? What sort of fixtures do you prefer? Do you like stall showers? Have you planned plenty of electrical outlets? How about an exercise terrace opening off your own bathroom? Would you like a small fireplace or electric heater?

Nursery

Do you want a fireplace here? (It's a very good place for one.) How about direct access to a playroof? Would a dumbwaiter direct from the kitchen or pantry be a step-saver? Have you placed this room on a sunny side of the house? Have you planned for plenty of closets for toys as well as clothes? Have you allowed a big closet for each child?

Special Storage

Where do you plan to store summer furniture, luggage, winter bedding and winter clothes? Are you planning a cedar closet, or a special linen closet with trays, drawers and shelves? Would a small closet equipped with a sink upstairs simplify your cleaning? Where are you going to keep big things like bicycles, baby carriages, garden tools, lawn mower?

Miscellaneous

How do you want to use the space in your cellar not taken up by the heating equpment? Do you want a storeroom—a game room—a drying room for clothes on rainy days—a cool room for vegetables—a wine cellar—a flower room that has access to out-of-doors?

Of course you've checked on air conditioning.

Do you want any special soundproofing, or fire prevention measures, or a burglar alarm system? Have you planned a system of bells throughout the house?

Are you absolutely sure that you have enough electric outlets all over the house? Do you want to install special indirect lighting anywhere?

Have you studied the placement of your radiators carefully?

Have you made a complete furniture layout before accepting the final plans from your architect?

Week-end or Hobby Houses

PERHAPS you've already built your house, and love it. Or perhaps you're not quite ready to build on a big, permanent scale. In either case, you might very well be tempted by a smaller building venture—a miniature week-end house in the country, or a hobby house built close to your big house.

Your week-end house might very well be a little French Provincial cottage, with one big, low living room and bedrooms no larger than the staterooms on a boat. Or you might want to do something as inexpensive and informal as the Saturday-night house described at the end of Chapter 13.

If you prefer something more sophisticated you might like a small but precise Regency house built on almost modern lines, with white plaster walls and a flat roof.

You might decide to spurn the land entirely and spend your summer week ends on a houseboat, anchored in some quiet inlet. Or you could get almost the same seafaring effect by remodeling a boathouse.

If you already have a big, comfortable house you may want to build yourself a separate study. This could be a circular library, two stories high and circled by a balcony. If music happens to be your hobby a small organ or piano would turn this into a retreat for the gods!

Or how about a tennis house, if that's your sport, built right beside the court? To be perfect, this would need a small but pleasant living room, a comfortable porch where spectators could watch the play, a simple kitchenette so that you could serve iced tea or lemonade and a couple of showers and tiny dressing rooms.

Whatever your country plans may be, there is one plea I would like to make—don't forget the country itself! Plan your out-of-door living right along with your house. Do you want a sunny dining terrace, an aviary, a greenhouse opening off the living room, a garden house, cold-frames for violets, keep bees or pigeons? If you do, now's the time to think about them. So, no matter how big or how small your building venture, think it all through with real care. Go over all the questions I have listed, sort out those that apply to you and add those I've omitted. Then when you go to your architect with all those questions organized in your mind he will probably faint dead away with surprise and joy. But when he rallies I guarantee that you will become fast friends and build exactly the house you've wanted all your life.

And when your house is finished you will have the incomparable fun of decorating it. I said at the beginning of this chapter that before I became a decorator and designer I built three houses for myself. I may as well admit now that the main reason I built three was because I loved decorating them so much. Try it yourself and I know you'll see why I had such a good time. Just as long as you put courage before conventionality and imagination before money decorating really *is* the best fun in the world.

Dorothy Draper
Hampshire House
New York, N. Y.

BIBLIOGRAPHY

MAGAZINES

Magazine	*Publisher*
Vogue	Condé Nast Publications 420 Lexington Ave. New York, N. Y.
House & Garden	Condé Nast Publications 420 Lexington Ave. New York, N. Y.
House Beautiful	Hearst Magazines, Inc. 572 Madison Ave. New York, N. Y.
Architectural Forum	Time and Life Building Rockefeller Center New York, N. Y.
Architectural Record	119 West 40th St. New York, N. Y.
American Home	251 Fourth Ave. New York, N. Y.

PAMPHLETS

The American Home also publishes the following useful pamphlets:

The American Home Portfolio of Period Furniture	50¢
The American Home Book of House Plans	$1.00
Summer Camp and Log Cabin Plans	25¢
Smart Interiors	$1.00
How to Make Your Own Slip Covers and Draperies	25¢
The Origin of Present Day Architecture	20¢
The American Home Architectural Portfolios	25¢
The Handy Man's Book	35¢
Things to Make Yourself	35¢
The American Home Book on Remodeling	35¢
Gardening Indoors and Flower Arrangements	50¢

Good Housekeeping Bulletin Service, 57th Street at Eighth Ave., New York, N. Y.
Pamphlets published to cover many different fields of study. List of pamphlets on request.
The Modern Homemaker, McCall's Magazine, Dayton, Ohio.
Booklets and leaflets of every type. Write to the above address for a list.
Create-a-Home Kit, The Bride's Magazine, 527 Fifth Ave., New York, N. Y.
The kit contains: 1. Full Instruction Sheets; 2. Floor Plans and Walls for three main rooms—living room, bedroom, dining room; 3. 31 Typical Doors and Windows; 4. Scaled Furniture Cut-Outs for 3 Rooms; 5. Shopping List and Swatch Sheet; 6. Scale Ruler; 7. Three Sheets of Decorating Ideas for Brides. Price, $1.00.

PRACTICAL CORRESPONDENCE COURSES

The New York School of Interior Decoration, 515 Madison Ave., New York, N. Y.
A practical and informative correspondence course for the student who wishes to study at home. The pupil is given a grounding in furniture layouts and period furniture. Practical training course, twenty lessons or practical training course and advanced course, twenty-six lessons. Booklet on request.
Practical Home Study Course in Interior Decoration, Edited by Arts and Decoration, 116 East 16th St., New York, N. Y.
Inclusive home-study course under an excellent board of directors. The course stresses historical styles and periods; also six lessons covering modern decoration. Many valuable supplements furnished the student. Thirty lessons. Booklet on request.
Successful Modern Living, Dorothy Draper, Inc., 38 East 57th St., New York, N. Y.
A short personal-correspondence course under Dorothy Draper for the woman of the modern world. The course covers such matters as—how to select the right decorative background for your personality; how to become a successful hostess; how to dress and spend smartly. A series of usable and practical lessons with individual counsel. Booklet on request.

For Those Who Are Seriously Interested:

I'm adding a short list of books that I've found useful. I don't think anything can give you as much pleasure as a library of books that you really like. Why not start to collect your favorites? If you can't do this right away, you can ask your local librarian to send to the state library for those you can't get at your home library. In this way you can find out whether you really want to purchase the book you are interested in. Some of them are very expensive and you'll want to know just what you're buying. I think it is fun to know as much as possible about one subject. It may be Queen Anne chairs or Early American silver, or merely the sort of hardware that was used on Louis XVI furniture. Decoration is full of "small" subjects to be interested in. Do choose one—you'll never be bored!

AMERICAN WORK

Lost Examples of American Architecture, John Mead Howells. William Helburn, Inc., New York, N. Y., 1931

All the buildings pictured have been destroyed or so altered that they are spoiled. This makes us realize how charmingly we once built and how slow we are to appreciate what we have. If you're building, or interested in old houses, this is a good book to have.

The White Pine Series of Architectural Monographs, Edited by Russell W. Whitehead, New York, N. Y.

This goes on and on. Almost everything in America must have been covered once. No one book could give you as much information. The photographs are excellent, and in the later issues there are good measured drawings.

Philip Hooker, Edward W. Root. Charles Scribner's Sons, New York, N. Y., 1929

The work of a little-known architect. Photographs and drawings. Some of the houses are charming, particularly Hyde Hall and the Miller House.

The Domestic Architecture of the Early American Republic
The Greek Revival, Howard Major. J. P. Lippincott, Philadelphia, Pa., 1926

Pages and pages of photographs of one of my favorite periods. All sections of the country are represented, so that you can see and study the originals. What could be nicer than a house done in this typically American style?

The Story of Architecture in America, Thomas E. Tallmadge. W. W. Norton & Co., New York, N. Y., 1927

Not many pictures, but the text is easily read and informative. This is one of the most painless books I know: you learn a lot with very little heavy reading. If you're interested in the story of our architecture and the people who made it, get this book.

The Early Architecture of Western Pennsylvania, William Helburn, Inc., New York, N. Y., 1936

From log houses to 1860. Numerous photographs and measured drawings. Some of the houses are lovely, and are full of ideas for the person who is going to build. If you live anywhere in the part of the country covered, I should think you'd certainly want this book. Some of the things have an elegance that we usually think of belonging only to the seaboard work.

A Handbook of the American Wing, R. T. H. Halsey and Charles O. Cornelius. Published by the Metropolitan Museum, New York, N. Y.

Good photographs of American furniture and rooms. The text is rather learned.

Monograph on the Work of Frank Lloyd Wright, The Architectural Forum for January, 1938

An issue of the *Architectural Forum* entirely devoted to the new and unpublished work of the distinguished American architect who has had more honor in other countries than in his own. By now it has been well established that Frank Lloyd Wright led the way in all the postwar European architectural developments. How strange that we should have been so long in recognizing his genius!

While I don't always agree with his interior treatments, the houses are exciting. The Kaufmann house in particular is really superb.

Space for Living: Creative Interior Decoration and Design, Paul T. Frankl. Doubleday, Doran & Co., New York, N. Y., 1938
An interesting book stressing modern furniture and decorative backgrounds.

The Geography of American Antiques, Laurelle Van Arsdale Guild. Doubleday, Doran & Co., New York, N. Y., 1927
A comprehensive study of American furniture.

ENGLISH WORK

Sir John Vanbrugh, Architect and Dramatist, Laurence Whistler. Cobden-Sanderson, London, 1938
A charmingly written "small" book about a colorful figure. Vanbrugh turned from drama to architecture and produced some astonishing houses. While the houses couldn't be copied, his sense of scale and drama in a house is something that we all could profit by.

English Domestic Architecture of the 17th and 18th Centuries, Horace Field and Michael Bunney. G. Bell and Sons, London, 1929
Photographs and measured drawings of small houses and outbuildings. I think it would be very useful to anyone about to build, and an easy start in the study of English architecture.

Late Georgian Houses (2 Volumes), Ramsey and Harvey. Architectural Press, London, 1923
One volume is given over to the exteriors, the other to details and interiors. The houses are a little more sophisticated than those in the preceding book. I found it delightful, and full of houses that I would like to live in.

A History of the English House, Nathaniel Lloyd. William Helburn, Inc., New York, N. Y., 1931
This is a "big" book, jammed with pictures of everything from the earliest times to Victorian work. Everything is covered—exteriors, plans, interiors, doors, windows, chimney pieces, gates, etc. A very useful reference work. The text is easily written, so that any amateur can understand what is being said.

The "English Homes" Series, C. Avery Tipping. Country Life, London, 1921
There are a great many volumes in this series which deals with houses that haven't been recorded before. I find one of the most useful the Early Georgian one (1714-1760). Good photographs, the "story" of the house and the people who built it, and notes on the architects, when they are known.

English Furniture from Charles II to George II, R. W. Symonds. International Studio, Inc., New York, N. Y., 1929
Lovely photographs of the loveliest furniture in the world. A perfect guide for you who are buying antiques, and a good yardstick with which to measure reproductions.

English Furniture from Gothic to Sheraton, Herbert Cescinsky. Dean-Hicks, Grand Rapids, Mich., 1929.

Everything in the world is here. If you want quick, painless knowledge, this is
the book for you.

FRENCH WORK

The Smaller Houses and Gardens of Versailles 1680–1815, Leigh French, Jr and
Harold Donaldson Eberlein. Pencil Points Press, New York, N. Y., 1926
   Photographs, plans and some measured drawings of the most enchanting houses.
I think this should be in every library. There are notes on the houses and their
gardens. The photographs are so good that any architect should be able to work
from them.
French Provincial Architecture, Philip Lippincott Goodwin and Henry Gothout
Milliken. Charles Scribner's Sons, New York, N. Y., 1924
   A beautiful book, with photographs and measured drawings. There are notes
on each of the houses. If you're going to build a French house, there isn't a better
book for you to consult.
French Provincial Furniture, Henri Longon and Frances Wilson Huard. J. P. Lippincott Co., Philadelphia, Pa., 1927
   The furniture of the provinces is taken up in separate chapters. Good illustrations from old prints and photographs. A book that should be used as a buying
guide, and for knowledge too.
Old French Furniture and Its Surroundings, Elisa Maillard. Charles Scribner's
Sons, New York, N. Y., 1925
   Photographs, drawings and old prints give you a pretty complete picture of the
furniture of France from 1610 to 1815. The text takes up the decoration of the
backgrounds, the sort of materials used for curtains and upholstery and the floor
coverings that were popular.
Louis XIV and Regency Furniture and Decoration, Seymour de Ricci. William
Helburn, Inc., New York, N. Y., 1929
   More than four hundred pictures of the "grandest" period of French architecture and decoration. While you won't want (or be able) to copy any of it,
the pictures are a good education. The introduction gives you enough information
to make you want more. A great many of the examples shown are now owned by
the Metropolitan Museum, so they may be seen as well as studied in the book.
Towards a New Architecture, Le Corbusier. Payson and Clarke, Ltd., New
York, N. Y.
   An interesting book that will make you think along the new lines of modern
architecture. Written by one of the great leaders of what might be called the
"functional" type of architecture.

OTHER COUNTRIES

Old Domestic Architecture of Holland, Edited by F. R. Yerbury. The Architectural Press, London, 1924
   This makes you wonder why we all don't build Dutch houses. Some of them
are utterly enchanting. There are a few interiors and drawings. If you can't build

a whole house, there are lots of ideas for garden houses, playhouses, garages, etc.

Bermuda Houses, John S. Humphreys. Marshall Jones Co., Boston, Mass., 1923

By now we all know Bermuda and its houses. This is full of photographs of the nicest ones. I've always thought that these houses were delightful because you could have a rambling "romantic" house combined with really "grand" Georgian details.

Modern Danish Architecture, Edited by Kay Fisker and F. R. Yerbury. Charles Scribner's Sons, New York, N. Y., 1927

While some of these are public buildings, there are enough private houses to make it worth your while. The houses look rather like Georgian or French houses but with all the ornament brushed off. Some of the interior details are fascinating —great shells over doors, flush wood walls with flush doors, etc.

Empire-und Beidermeirmobel, Ferdinand Luthmer and Robert Schmidt. Julius Hoffmann, Stuttgart, 1922

Furniture and interiors of the German Empire period. I think some of the furniture is beautiful, and some of it has an absolutely modern quality. For those of you who like a rather stylized background this will be of real interest. (Written in German.)

The Practical Book of Italian, Spanish and Portuguese Furniture, Harold Donaldson Eberlein and Roger Wearne Ramsdell. J. B. Lippincott Co., Philadelphia, Pa., 1927

Despite the rather grim title, this book has lots of good photographs of furniture of all periods. The text takes up the backgrounds and decorative treatments. You should find it useful as a check when buying either antiques or reproductions.

Majorcan Houses and Gardens, Arthur Bryne and Mildred Stapley. William Helburn, Inc., 1928

Full of pictures of romantic houses and gardens, tile roofs, patios, etc.

Mobilier et Décoration des Anciens Palais Imperiaux Russes, G.-K. Loukomski. Les Éditions G. Van Oest, Paris et Bruxelles, 1928

If any of you have been in any doubt of the elegance of decoration in prewar Russia here is the book that will make you change your mind. Some of the things are astonishing—walls of porcelain, superb furniture, lovely inlaid floors. Again, you couldn't *copy* any of it, but it is full of ideas. Try translating one of the wood floors to linoleum or zenitherm, some of the gilded plaster wall decorations to paint. A valuable book for your library. (Written in French.)

Swedish Architecture of the Twentieth Century, Ahlberg. Charles Scribner's Sons, New York, N. Y., 1925

Mostly public buildings but full of ideas. A perfect style for the person building in a northern climate—shiny roofs, soft colored walls, boldly patterned floors to be used with modern or Empire furniture.

SPECIAL SUBJECTS

Historic Wallpapers, Nancy V. McClelland. J. B. Lippincott Co., Philadelphia, Pa., 1924.

I think this must be the "standard" work on wallpaper. Lots of illustrations, a few in color. The text takes up the history and development of wall coverings. An invaluable book.

The Old Chintz Book, Maciver Percival. William Heinemann, Ltd., London, 1923
    A charming small book all about chintz—a subject close to my heart! Four colored plates and a number of others in black and white. The designs are lovely.

German Baroque Sculpture, Sacherverell Sitwell and Anthony Ayscough. Duckworth, London, 1938
    Excellent photographs of little-known things. The subject, you may feel, is a little special, but this is a good approach to an important period about which little has been written in English.

Historical Colours, Thomas Parsons & Sons, Ltd., London. 1934. This and also the two books listed below are invaluable for decorative paint samples.

Han'tec Color Book, Sigrid K. Lonegren, 630 Fifth Ave., New York, N. Y.

Color Combinations, William Helburn, Inc., 15 East 55th St., New York, N. Y.

ACKNOWLEDGMENTS

The drawings in this book have been prepared by Lester Grundy. All the rooms shown in the photographs are the work of the office of Dorothy Draper, Inc. Credit is also given to *Collier's* for the photographs by Robert Yarnall Richie of the *One-Room Apartment* and *A Living Room*; to Van Nes-De Vos for *Twin Four-Posters, Table Set From the Five-and-Ten-Cent Store, and Bedroom Details*; to Drix Duryea, Inc., for the photograph *Dramatic Front Hall* and to Nyholm for the photograph *Dinner for Eight* (Copyright, 1936, The Condé Nast Publications, Inc.); to Pittsburgh Plate Glass Co. for *Living Room in a Remodeled Country House*.

INDEX